Modern Critical Interpretations

William Wordsworth's
The Prelude

Modern Critical Interpretations

These and other titles in preparation

William Wordsworth's
The Prelude

Edited and with an introduction by
Harold Bloom
Sterling Professor of the Humanities
Yale University

CHELSEA HOUSE PUBLISHERS ◊ 1986
NEW YORK ◊ NEW HAVEN ◊ PHILADELPHIA

© 1986 by Chelsea House Publishers,
a division of Chelsea House Educational Communications, Inc.
133 Christopher Street, New York, NY 10014
345 Whitney Avenue, New Haven, CT 06511
5014 West Chester Pike, Edgemont, PA 19028

Printed and bound in the United States of America

∞ The paper used in this publication meets the minimum requirements of the
American National Standard for Permanence of Paper for Printed Library Materials, Z39.48–1984.

Library of Congress Cataloging-in-Publication Data
Main entry under title:
William Wordsworth—The Prelude.
  (Modern critical interpretations)
  Bibliography : p.
  Includes index.
  1. Wordsworth, William, 1770–1850. Prelude—Addresses, essays, lec-
tures. I. Bloom, Harold.
II. Series.
PR5864.W67 1986   821'.7   85-29107
ISBN 0–87754–749–1

Contents

Editor's Note

This book gathers together a representative selection of the best modern criticism devoted to Wordsworth's masterwork, *The Prelude*, by common consent the principal long poem in the language since Milton's *Paradise Lost*. The critical essays are arranged here in the chronological order of their original publication, except for the editor's introduction, which first appeared in 1961. I am grateful to Susan Lasher for her valuable assistance in editing this volume.

The introduction provides a comprehensive overview of the whole of *The Prelude*, with emphasis upon the poem's relationship to Wordsworth's most significant shorter poems. William Empson's highly characteristic study of "Sense in *The Prelude*" begins the chronological sequence with an intense analysis of the structure of a complex word that initially appears to be simple and even rather flat. This formalistic approach is complemented by Donald Davie's equally rigorous account of syntax in *The Prelude*'s blank verse, which is seen to depend for its suppleness and rhetorical power on Wordsworth's mastery over his transitive verbs.

A very different mode of criticism is introduced here by Geoffrey Hartman's acute exegesis of Wordsworth's negations in his Romantic quest for nature. Hartman is the dominant modern critic in what can be called A. C. Bradley's tradition of Wordsworthian study, as opposed to Matthew Arnold's view, which is most strongly espoused by M. H. Abrams in our time. Bradley emphasized Wordsworth as a poet of the Sublime, while Arnold's Wordsworth was *the* poet of Nature. Hartman's Wordsworth seeks his own imaginative autonomy in regard to nature, while guarding against yielding too fully to the impulse that might leap over nature into the consummation of a personal apocalypse. Herbert Lindenberger, whose stance towards Wordsworth can be said to mediate between Bradley and

Arnold, is represented here by a sensitive reading of the "Spots of Time" passages as structural units necessary for us to apprehend, if we are not to lose the art of reading a long poem.

With the exegesis by M. H. Abrams of what he calls "Wordsworth's Long Journey Home," we are in the presence of a highly sophisticated Arnoldian view of *The Prelude* as an imaginative displacement of theological and metaphysical truths into the language of poetry. An immediate contrast to Abrams is provided in Richard J. Onorato's Freudian reading of the self in *The Prelude*. Onorato's Freudianism is essentially that of the American school of Ego Psychology (Heinz Hartmann, Kris, Erikson) and is complemented here by Robert Young's Lacanian analysis, with its very different insistence that the ego itself is largely unconscious. Young sees the driving impulse of any poem as being the force of unconscious desire.

Newer modes of rhetorical study, akin to Young's Lacanian deconstructions, are present also in David E. Simpson's rather severe remarks upon the "Spots of Time" as "spaces for refiguring," in which Wordsworth can address himself again to his complex program of revitalizing the ways in which poems can represent the problematical relations between the human and the natural. This book concludes with a distinguished instance of the newer criticism, the study by Mary Jacobus of some of the senses in which the rhetorical figure of apostrophe determines the movements of lyric voice in *The Prelude*.

Introduction

The Prelude, completed in 1805, was published after Wordsworth's death in 1850. The title was chosen by the poet's widow; for Wordsworth it was simply "the poem to Coleridge." The 1850 text both suffers and gains by nearly half a century of Wordsworth's revisions, for the poet of the decade 1798–1807 was not the Urizenic bard of the *Ecclesiastical Sonnets*, and the attempts of the older Wordsworth to correct the younger are not always fortunate. The 1850 text shows better craftsmanship, but it also sometimes manifests an orthodox censor at work, straining to correct a private myth into an approach at Anglican dogma. As Wordsworth's modern editor, Ernest de Selincourt, has observed, nothing could be more significant than the change of

> I worshipped then among the depths of things
> As my soul bade me...
> I felt and nothing else
>
> (XI, 234–8, 1805)

to

> Worshipping then among the depths of things
> As piety ordained...
> I felt, observed, and pondered
>
> (XII, 184–8, 1850)

In the transition between these two passages, Wordsworth loses his Miltonic heritage, an insistence upon the creative autonomy of the individual soul. With it he loses also an emphasis peculiar to himself, a reliance upon the *felt* experience, as distinguished from received piety or the abstraction that follows experience. In what follows I shall cite the 1850 text, but with reference, where it seems desirable, to the 1805 version.

The poem approximates epic structure, in that its fourteen books

1

gather to a climax after a historical series of progressively more vital crises and renovations. The first eight books form a single movement, summed up in the title of Book Eight, "Retrospect—Love of Nature Leading to Love of Mankind." Books Nine, Ten, and Eleven carry this Love of Mankind into its natural consequence, Wordsworth's "Residence in France," and his involvement with the Revolution. Books Twelve and Thirteen deal with the subsequent crisis of Wordsworth's "Imagination, How Impaired and Restored." The "Conclusion," Book Fourteen, is the climax of Wordsworth's imaginative life and takes the reader back, in a full cycle, to the very opening of the poem. The "Conclusion" presents Wordsworth and Coleridge as "Prophets of Nature," joint laborers in the work of man's redemption:

> what we have loved,
> Others will love, and we will teach them how;
> Instruct them how the mind of man becomes
> A thousand times more beautiful than the earth
> On which he dwells.

Blake, had he read this, would have approved, though he might have wondered where Wordsworth had accounted for that "thousand times more beautiful." Blake's distrust of Wordsworth's dialectics of Nature is to some extent confirmed by Wordsworth himself. "Natural objects always did and now do weaken, deaden, and obliterate imagination in me," was Blake's comment on Wordsworth's fragment "Influence of Natural Objects" . . . and Wordsworth does fall mute when the external stimulus is too clearly present. Geoffrey Hartman remarks that even in Wordsworth "poetry is not an act of consecration and Nature not an immediate external object to be consecrated." A natural object liberates Wordworth's imagination only when it both ceases to be purely external and fades out of its object status.

The romantic metaphor of the correspondent breeze has [previously] been discussed. The wind of Beulah, creative and destructive, rises in the opening lines of *The Prelude*. Wordsworth need not call upon this spirit, for it precedes his invocation. It begins as a gentle breeze, and a blessing, half-conscious of the joy it gives to the new Moses who has escaped the Egypt that is London, and new Adam who can say:

> The earth is all before me. With a heart
> Joyous, nor scared at its own liberty,
> I look about; and should the chosen guide
> Be nothing better than a wandering cloud,
> I cannot miss my way.

Adam and Eve, scarcely joyous, go out hand in hand as loving children into all that is before them to choose a place of rest, with the Divine Providence as their guide. Wordsworth seeks a place where he will be lulled into the creative repose of epic composition, and he picks his own guide; nor need it be a Mosaic pillar, for he cannot miss his way. Nature, all before him, is generous, and his choice can only be between varying modes of good. *The Prelude* therefore opens without present anxiety: its crises are in the past. Unlike *Paradise Lost* and Blake's *Jerusalem, The Prelude* is a song of triumph rather than a song of experience. Wordsworth sings of what Blake called "organized innocence."

When the wind blows upon Wordsworth, he feels within a corresponding breeze, which rapidly becomes:

> A tempest, a redundant energy,
> Vexing its own creation.

Wordsworth's account of this vexing redundancy is that he is:

> not used to make
> A present joy the matter of a song

Although he tries again, aided by Eolian visitations, his harmony disperses in straggling sounds and, lastly, utter silence. What matters is his reaction. There is no despair, no sense of loss, only a quiet confidence based upon the belief that his inspiration is henceforward to be perpetual:

> "Be it so;
> Why think of anything but present good?"

We mistake *The Prelude*, then, if we seek to find a crisis, rather than the history of a crisis, within it. *The Prelude* is not a tragic poem but an autobiographical myth-making. Dominating *The Prelude* is the natural miracle of memory as an instrumentality by which the self is saved. Supreme among Wordsworth's inventions is the myth of renovating "spots of time," crucial in the "Intimations" ode and "Tintern Abbey," and the entire basis for the imaginative energy of *The Prelude*.

The story of *The Prelude* is mysterious only in that Wordsworthian Nature is now a mystery to most of us. For Wordsworth, Nature is first of all the sensuous *given*—what is freely offered for our discernment at all times. Like Blake, Wordsworth is preeminently a master of phenomenology, in the sense that he is able to read reality in appearances. Like Abraham, Wordsworth is the patriarch of a Covenant, made in the latter case between phenomenal appearance and the human heart. If the human heart, in its common, everyday condition, will love and trust the phenomenal world, then that world will never betray it. Betrayal here takes some of the force of its meaning from the context of sexuality and marriage. For man to betray Nature is to embrace one of the several modes in which the primacy of Imagination is denied. For Nature to betray man is to cease as a renovating virtue for man when he returns to it. Man turns from that loving embrace of nature which *is* in fact the supreme act of the Imagination, and takes the cruel mistress of discursiveness in her place. Nature turns from man by ceasing to be a Beulah state, and becoming instead a hostile and external object. What Wordsworth never considers is the more sinister manifestation of Nature-as-temptress, Blake's Vala or Keats's Belle Dame. Shelley climaxes his heritage from the Wordsworth tradition in "The Triumph of Life" by introducing Wordsworthian Nature as the deceptive "Shape all light," who tramples the divine sparks of Rousseau's imagination into the dust of death. Wordsworth's symbol of the covenant between man and nature, the rainbow, is employed by Shelley as the emblem that precedes the appearance of the beautiful but destructive Nature figure of "The Triumph of Life."

The inner problem of *The Prelude*, and of all the poetry of Wordsworth's great decade, is that of the autonomy of the poet's creative imagination. Indeed, as we have seen, it is the single most crucial problem of all that is most vital in English Romantic poetry. Even Wordsworth, the prophet of Nature, is uneasy at the prospect of his spirit's continual dependence upon it. He insists, like all prophets in the Hebraic tradition, upon the mutual dependence of the spiritual world and its human champion. The correspondent breeze is necessary because of natural decay; our mortality insists upon being redeemed by our poetry. To serve Nature in his early years, Wordsworth needed only to be wisely passive. But to sustain himself (and Nature?) in his maturity, an initiative from within is required. And yet if the initiative is too overt, as here at the opening of *The Prelude*, then Nature refuses to be so served, and the mutual creation that is the poem cannot go forward.

Hartman, analyzing this problem, says that "Nature keeps the initiative. The mind at its most free is still part of a deep mood of weathers." Wordsworth's problem is thus a dialectical one, for what he seeks is the proper first term that will yield itself readily to be transcended. The first term is not Poetry, for Nature at *The Prelude*'s onset will not have it so. Nor can the first term be Nature, for it will not allow itself to be subsumed even by the naturalizing imagination, at least *not immediately*. Blake has no patience for the Primary Imagination, but the whole of the secret discipline of Wordsworth's art is to wait upon it, confident that it will at last consent to dissolve into a higher mode.

Hartman speaks of the difficult first term of Wordsworth's dialectic as being "neither Nature nor Poetry. It is, rather, Imagination in embryo—muted yet strengthened by Nature's inadequacies." This is certainly the best balance to keep, unless we consent to a more radical review of Wordsworth's doctrine of Nature. Gorky said of Tolstoy's dealings with God that they reminded him of the old proverb "two bears in one den," and one can say the same of Wordsworth's relations with Nature. After a time, there is not quite room for both of them in Wordsworth's poetry if either is to survive full-size, and clearly it is Nature that makes room for Wordsworth. Yet the struggle, while concealed, inhibits Wordsworth and limits his achievement. There are unresolved antagonisms between Poetry and Divinity in Milton, but nothing so prolonged as the hidden conflict between Poetry and Nature in Wordsworth. But for this conflict, Wordsworth might have attempted national epic. Because of it, he was compelled to work in the mode of Rousseau, the long confessional work that might clarify his relation both to Nature and his own poetic calling.

The Nature of *The Prelude* is what Wordsworth was to become, a great teacher. Nature is so strong a teacher that it first must teach itself the lesson of restraint, to convert its immediacy into a presence only lest it overpower its human receiver. Wordsworth desires it as a mediating presence, a motion and a spirit. When it *is* too powerful, it threatens to become first, an object of worship, and second, like all such objects, an exhaustible agent of reality, a life that can be drained. Wordsworth knows well the dangers of idolatry, the sinister dialectic of mutual use. He desires only a relationship, a moment-to-moment confrontation of life by life, a dialogue. In this respect he is the direct ancestor of Shelley's vision of Nature.

The Prelude tries to distinguish between the *immediate* and the *remembered* external worlds. It is the paradoxical freedom of the Wordsworthian Imagination that it must avoid bondage to the immediate but seek the reign of the remembered world. In Blake the Imagination strives to be totally free of both, externals and memory, and delights only in the final excellence, the imagined land. Blake has no quest; only a struggle against everything within and without himself that is not pure Imagination. But Wordsworth has the quest that Blake's marginalia upon him gave clear warning of, the search for the autonomy of his own imagination. Hartman suggests that Nature's particular grace toward Wordsworth is to unfold *gradually* his own freedom to him, as his quest is largely an unwilling one; he does not want to be free of Nature. This suggestion is a displaced form of the Christian reading of history; for Wordsworth's "Nature" read St. Augustine's "History," as both are varieties of mercy presented as gradualism.

The hidden tragedy running through *The Prelude* is Wordsworth's resistance to his own imaginative emancipation. Wordsworth has clues enough, but usually declines to read them. In the presence of too eloquent a natural image, he is speechless. Nor does he attempt, after "Tintern Abbey," to particularize any local habitations for vision. He diffuses the secret strength of things over the widest possible landscape, in contrast to his disciple Shelley, who stands before Mont Blanc and cries "The power is there." Again, unlike their operations in Shelley and in Blake, the epiphanies in Wordsworth are not really sudden; there are no raptures of prophecy, but rather a slowly mounting intensity of baffled vision until at last the illumination greatly comes.

For Blake, and finally for Shelley, the Imagination's freedom from Nature is a triumph. It makes Wordsworth profoundly uneasy; he does not believe that time and space ought to be abandoned quite so prematurely. For Blake, the matter of common perception, the world of Primary Imagination, is hindrance, not action, but for Wordsworth it is something better than action; it is contemplation, and to see something clearly is already to have made some sense out of the diffuse and chaotic world of sensation. To mold a few of these clear things into a simpler and still clearer unity is to have made imaginative sense out of sensation. Blake's protest is absolute. He saw both these operations as passive, as a surrender to the living death of a world too small to contain the expansive vision of a more human Man.

The world of *The Prelude* is exquisitely fitted to the individual mind of the young Wordsworth. Even when it works upon him by frustration or fear, it continues to teach the young poet. The passages at the opening of the poem concerning the frustrating of composition have been examined above. Though he puts aside these failures, which are due to the immediacy of his inspiration, he is more troubled by the greater frustration of seemingly finding no subject for sustained epic. Even this vacant musing is redeemed by Nature, for in reproving himself he is carried back into remembrances, and these not only give him his only proper subject but begin the genuine forward movement of his poem. The growth of a poet's mind, as fostered by the goodly universe around him, becomes the inevitable subject as he sustains a gentle self-chastisement:

> Was it for this
> That one, the fairest of all rivers, loved
> To blend his murmurs with my nurse's song.

As the Derwent river once flowed along his dreams, now it stirs a flow of memory, carrying the mature poet back into the salvation of things past. The image of the coursing river runs through the entire poem, and provides the analogue for the flowing progress of the long work. Wordsworth speaks of "the river of my mind," and warns that its portions cannot be traced to individual fountains, but rather to the whole flow of the sensuous generosity of external phenomena.

The first two books of the poem show the child as encountering unknown modes of being, the life of Nature which is both one with us and yet dwells apart in its tranquillity. The primordial strength of Wordsworth's mind, its closeness to the myth-makings of early cultures and of children, is revealed in the incident in which an early wrong-doing is followed by hints of natural nemesis:

> and when the deed was done
> I heard among the solitary hills
> Low breathings coming after me, and sounds
> Of undistinguishable motion, steps
> Almost as silent as the turf they trod.

We make a mistake if we read this as a projection of the child's conscience upon the external world. That he heard it is warrant enough for its reality. Similarly, when he hangs above the raven's nest, sustained by the grip of finger tips, he hears a strange utterance in the wind, and perceives a motion unlike any ordinary one, in a sky that does not seem a sky of earth. At such a moment he belongs more to the universe of elemental forces, of motions and spirits, than he does to ours.

These early incidents of participation in other modes of being climax in the famous episode of the stolen boat, "an act of stealth and troubled pleasure." There is a muffled sexual element in this boyish escapade. The moon shines on the child as he lustily dips his oars into the silent lake. Suddenly, from behind a craggy steep that had been till then the horizon's bound:

> a huge peak, black and huge,
> As if with voluntary power instinct,
> Upreared its head.

The grim shape, with its own purpose and the measured motion of a living thing, comes striding after him. He flees, returns the boat, and for many days is haunted by a sense of "unknown modes of being":

> No familiar shapes
> Remained, no pleasant images of trees,
> Of sea or sky, no colours of green fields;
> But huge and mighty forms, that do not live
> Like living men, moved slowly through the mind
> By day, and were a trouble to my dreams.

This is a fundamental paganism, so primitive that it cannot yield to any more sophisticated description without distortion. It is like the Titanism of Blake, with its Giant Forms like the Zoas wandering a world substantially our own. Worth particular attention is the momentary withdrawal of the given world of Nature from the boy, for it hints that familiar natural beauty is a gift, not to be retained by the unnatural.

The theme of reciprocity is introduced in this passage and strengthened by the skating incident, where the giving of one's body to the wind is repaid by being allowed to see, in a sense, the motion of earth in her diurnal round.

Summing up the first book, Wordsworth sees his mind as revived, now that he has found "a theme / Single and of determined bounds." Yet the most vital passage of the second book breaks beyond bounds, and makes clear how ultimately ambitious the theme is:

> and I would stand,
> If the night blackened with a coming storm,
> Beneath some rock, listening to notes that are
> The ghostly language of the ancient earth,
> Or make their dim abode in distant winds.
> Thence did I drink the visionary power

Listening to the wind is a mode of primitive augury, but it is not gross prophecy of the future that the boy aspires toward as he hears the primordial language of earth. The exultation involved, Wordsworth goes on to say, is profitable, not because of its content:

> but that the soul,
> Remembering how she felt, but what she felt
> Remembering not, retains an obscure sense
> Of possible sublimity, whereto
> With growing faculties she doth aspire,
> With faculties still growing, feeling still
> That whatsoever point they gain, they yet
> Have something to pursue.

No passage in *The Prelude* is more central, and nothing is a better description of Wordsworth's poetry. *What* his soul felt in different encounters with Nature, he will not always remember. *How* it felt is recalled, and this retains that obscure sense of possible sublimity that colors all of the poetry of the Great Decade. As the soul's faculties grow, the soul is in danger of becoming content, of ceasing to aspire, but is saved from such sleep by the sense of possible sublimity. This sublimity, in its origins, has little to do with love or sympathy for others, and has small relation to human suffering. It is a sense of individual greatness, of a joy and a light yet unknown even in the child's life. *The Prelude*, until the eighth book, devotes itself largely to an inward world deeply affected only by external nature, but with a gradually intensifying sense of others held just in abeyance.

The soul in solitude moves outward by encountering other solitaries. Solitude, Wordsworth writes in Book Four, is most potent when impressed upon the mind with an appropriate human center. Having escorted a wandering old soldier to shelter, Wordsworth entreats him to linger no more on the roads, but instead to ask for the help that his state requires. With a "ghastly mildness" on his face the vagrant turns back the reproof:

> "My trust is in the god of Heaven,
> And in the eye of him who passes me!"

From this first lesson in human reciprocity, Wordsworth's narrative flows inward again, but this time to make clear the imaginative relation between Nature and literature (Book Five), which centers on a dream of apocalypse and survival. Sitting by the seaside, reading *Don Quixote*, he begins to muse on poetry and mathematics as being the ultimate apprehenders of reality, and having the "high privilege of lasting life." He falls asleep, and dreams. Around him is a boundless, sandy, wild plain, and distress and fear afflict him, till a Bedouin appears upon a dromedary. He bears a lance, and carries a stone beneath one arm, and holds a shell of surpassing brightness in the opposite hand. The Arab tells him that the stone is "Euclid's Elements" and the shell "is something of more worth," poetry. When Wordsworth puts the shell to his ear, as commanded, he hears:

> A loud prophetic blast of harmony;
> An Ode, in passion uttered, which foretold
> Destruction to the children of the earth
> By deluge, now at hand.

The Arab's mission is to bury "these two books," stone and shell, against the day when the flood shall recede. The poet attempts to join him in this enterprise, but he hurries off. Wordsworth follows, baffled because the Arab now looks like Don Quixote, then an Arab again, and then "of these was neither, and was both at once." The waters of the deep gather upon them, but in the aspect of "a bed of glittering light." Wordsworth wakes in terror, to view the sea before him and the book at his side.

The dream is beautifully suggestive, and invites the kind of symbol-building that W. H. Auden performs with it in his lively exercise in Romantic iconography, *The Enchafèd Flood*. Unlike the use of water symbolism in most of Wordsworth, the deluge here threatens both Imagination and abstract reason, and the semi-Quixote flees the waters of judgment that Wordsworth, like the prophet Amos, elsewhere welcomes. Wordsworth puts Imagination at the water line in the marvelous passage about the children sporting on the shore which provides the "Intimations" ode with its liberating epiphany. The seashell participates in both the land of reasoning and the sea of apocalypse, of primal unity, which makes it an ideal type of the poetic Imagination. Though the Arab says that the shell is of more worth than the stone, the passage clearly sets high value on geometric as well as instinctual truth. Yet the stone as a symbol for mathematical reason is very close to Blake's Urizenic symbolism; the Ulro is associated with slabs of stone. Wallace Stevens's use of "the Rock" as symbol is closer to Wordsworth in spirit. The Rock, like the stone, is the gray particular of man's life, which poetry must cause to flower.

One can either pursue an investigation of the dream properties in this incident, which is endless, or else turn to Wordsworth's own reading of it, which takes us closer again to the design of *The Prelude*. The most important point is how close Wordsworth comes to identifying himself with the Arab Quixote. He fancies him a living man, "crazed by love and feeling, and internal thought protracted among endless solitudes." This is a fate that Wordsworth feared for himself, had his sensibility taken too strong control of his reason. For the Arab's mission, though the poet calls it mad, "that maniac's fond anxiety," is very like Wordsworth's own in *The Prelude*. Both desire to save Imagination from the abyss of desert and ocean, man's solitary isolation from and utter absorption into Nature. But the Arab is quixotic; he pursues a quest that is hopeless, for the deluge will cover all. Wordsworth hopes that his own quest will bring the healing waters down, as he pursues his slow, flowing course toward his present freedom.

The first of the major breakthroughs of the Imagination in *The Prelude* comes soon after this dream. The poet, in Book Six, describes a summer expedition to the Alps. He desires to cross the Alps for reasons obscure even to himself. It may be a desire to emancipate his maturing Imagination from Nature by overcoming the greatest

natural barrier he can encounter. He draws an explicit parallel between his Alpine expedition and the onset of the French Revolution:

> But Nature then was sovereign in my mind,
> And mighty forms, seizing a youthful fancy,
> Had given a charter to irregular hopes.
> In any age of uneventful calm
> Among the nations, surely would my heart
> Have been possessed by similar desire;
> But Europe at that time was thrilled with joy,
> France standing on the top of golden hours,
> And human nature seeming born again.

The rebirth of human nature heralds Wordsworth's own "irregular hope." He does not seem conscious altogether of the personal
revolution he seeks to effect for his own imagination. He speaks of
it as "an underthirst," which is "seldom utterly allayed," and causes
a sadness different in kind from any other. To illustrate it, he cites
the incident of his actual crossing of the Alps. He misses his path,
and frustrates his "hopes that pointed to the clouds," for a peasant
informs him that he has crossed the Alps without even being aware
of the supposed achievement. This moment of baffled aspiration is
suddenly seen as the agent of a transfiguration:

> Imagination—here the Power so called
> Through sad incompetence of human speech,
> That awful Power rose from the mind's abyss
> Like an unfathered vapour that enwraps,
> At once, some lonely traveller.

The mind's thwarted expectation makes it a shapeless abyss; the
Imagination *rises from it,* and is self-begotten, like the sudden vapor,
"unfathered," that enwraps the lonely traveler. Yet the Imagination
remains ours, even if at the time of crisis it seems alien to us:

> I was lost;
> Halted without an effort to break through;
> But to my conscious soul I now can say—
> "I recognise thy glory"

The vertigo resulting from the gap between expectation and
fulfillment halts Wordsworth at the moment of his disappointment,
and leaves him without the will to transcend his frustration. But *now,*

in recollection, he recognizes the glory of the soul's triumphant faculty of expectation:

> in such strength
> Of usurpation, when the light of sense
> Goes out, but with a flash that has revealed
> The invisible world, doth greatness make abode,
> There harbours; whether we be young or old,
> Our destiny, our being's heart and home,
> Is with infinitude, and only there;
> With hope it is, hope that can never die,
> Effort, and expectation, and desire,
> And something evermore about to be.

Even here, in a passage bordering the realm of the mystical, the poet's emphasis is naturalistic. Imagination usurps the place of the baffled mind, and the light of sense momentarily goes out: that is, the object world is not perceived. *But*, and this proviso is the poet's, the flash of greater illumination that suddenly reveals the invisible world is itself due to the flickering light of sense. Nature is overcome by Nature, and the senses are transcended by a natural teaching. The transcendence is the vital element in this passage, for in the Imagination's strength to achieve transcendence is the abode and harbor of human greatness. "More! More! is the cry of a mistaken Soul. Less than All cannot satisfy Man," is Blake's parallel statement. Wordsworth stresses infinitude because he defines the imaginative as that which is conversant with or turns upon infinity. In a letter to the poet Landor (January 21, 1824) he defines an imaginative passage as one in which "things are lost in each other, and limits vanish, and aspirations are raised." To the earlier statement in *The Prelude* celebrating "an obscure sense of possible sublimity" (II, 317–8), we can add this passage's sense of "something evermore about to be." Such a sense constitutes for the soul its "banners militant," under which it seeks no trophies or spoils, no self-gratification, for it is:

> blest in thoughts
> That are their own perfection and reward,
> Strong in herself and in beatitude
> That hides her, like the mighty flood of Nile
> Poured from his fount of Abyssinian clouds
> To fertilise the whole Egyptian plain.

This is a tribute to the autonomy of the creative soul, and to its ultimate value as well. The soul in creation rises out of the unfathered vapor just as the flood of the Nile rises from its cloud-shrouded heights. The waters of creation pour down and fertilize the mind's abyss, giving to it something of the soul's strength of effort, expectation, and desire.

Directly after this revelation, Wordsworth is free to trace the "characters of the great Apocalypse." As he travels through a narrow chasm in the mountains, Nature reveals to him the unity between its constant outer appearances and the ultimate forms of eternity:

> The immeasurable height
> Of woods decaying, never to be decayed,
> The stationary blasts of waterfalls,
> And in the narrow rent at every turn
> Winds thwarting winds, bewildered and forlorn,
> The torrents shooting from the clear blue sky,
> The rocks that muttered close upon our ears,
> Black drizzling crags that spake by the way-side
> As if a voice were in them, the sick sight
> And giddy prospect of the raving stream,
> The unfettered clouds and region of the Heavens,
> Tumult and peace, the darkness and the light—
> Were all like workings of one mind, the features
> Of the same face, blossoms upon one tree;
> Characters of the great Apocalypse,
> The types and symbols of Eternity,
> Of first, and last, and midst, and without end.

So much is brought together so magnificently in this that we can read it as a summary of what the poet has to say about the final relation between phenomena and the invisible world. The woods are constantly in process of decay, but the process will never cease; it will continue into Apocalypse. The waterfalls descend, and yet give the appearance of being stationed where they are, not to be moved. The winds are antithetical, balancing one another in the narrow chasm. Thwarted, bewildered, forlorn; they are humanized by this description. Torrents, rocks, crags participate in this speaking with tongues, and the raving stream takes on attributes of human disorder. Above, the unbound Heavens contrast their peace to this torment, their light to this darkness. The above and the below are like the workings of one unified mind, and are seen as features of the same face, blossoms upon one tree, either and both together. For the human and the natural are alike characters of the great unveiling of reality, equal types and symbols of the everlasting. The power that moves Man is the power that impels Nature, and Man and Nature, taken together, are the true form, not to be transcended even by a last judgment. This intimation of survival is given to Wordsworth under Nature's guidance, but the point of revelation is more human than natural. What the poet describes here is not Nature but the force for which he lacks a name, and which is at one with that "something far more deeply interfused" celebrated in "Tintern Abbey."

After this height in Book Six, the poem descends into the abyss of residence in London in Book Seven.

Imagination rises for Wordsworth in solitude, and yet "Tintern Abbey" puts a very high value upon "the still, sad music of humanity," a love of men that depends upon societies. F. A. Pottle remarks of Wordsworth in this context that though the poet "had the best of intentions, he could never handle close-packed, present, human crowds in the mode of imagination. If he were to grasp the life of a great city imaginatively, it had to be at night or early in the morning, while the streets were deserted; or at least in bad weather, when few people were abroad." As Wordsworth goes along the overflowing street, he is oppressed by a sense that the face of everyone he passes is a mystery to him. Suddenly he is smitten with the view:

> Of a blind Beggar, who, with upright face,
> Stood, propped against a wall, upon his chest
> Wearing a written paper, to explain
> His story, whence he came, and who he was.
> Caught by the spectacle my mind turned round
> As with the might of waters

The huge fermenting mass of humankind does not set the poet's imagination in motion, but the sight of one solitary man among them does. Wordsworth says that the pathetic label the beggar wears is an apt type of the utmost we can know, either of the universe or of ourselves, but this is not the imaginative meaning of the Beggar's sudden manifestation. Like the old Leech Gatherer of "Resolution and Independence," he causes the mind to assume the condition of the moving waters of Apocalypse, to receive a hint of the final communion between Man and Nature. The Leech Gatherer does this merely by being what he is, a reduced but still human form thoroughly at peace in a landscape reduced to naked desolation, but still natural. The blind Beggar's landscape is the noise of the crowd around him. He sits "with upright face"; the detail suggests the inner uprightness, the endurance of the outwardly bent Leech Gatherer. Amid the shock for eyes and ears of what surrounds him, his label affords a silent vision of human separateness, of the mystery of individual being.

From this bleak image, the poet retires with joy in Book Eight, which both heralds his return to Nature and chronicles the course of the first half of the poem, the stages by which love of Nature has led to love for Man. The figure linking the first love to the second is the shepherd, endowed by the boy Wordsworth with mythical powers and incarnating the virtues of Natural Man, an Adam who needs no dying into life, no second birth. The shepherd affects his own domain by intensifying its own characteristics:

> I felt his presence in his own domain,
> As of a lord and master, or a power,
> Or genius, under Nature, under God,
> Presiding; and severest solitude
> Had more commanding looks when he was there.

This figure gives Wordsworth the support he needs for his "trust in what we *may* become." The shepherd, like Michael, like even the Old Cumberland Beggar, is a figure of capable imagination, strong in the tie that binds him to the earth.

Natural love for Man leads Wordsworth where it led the French followers of the prophet Rousseau, to Revolution in the name of the Natural Man. His particular friend in that cause, Michel Beaupuy (or Beaupuis, as Wordsworth spells it, Book Nine, line 419), fighting for the Revolution as a high officer, says to him on encountering a hunger-bitten girl, "'Tis against *that* that we are fighting." As simply, Wordsworth says of him: "Man he loved as man."

The 1850 *Prelude* omits the tragic story of Wordsworth's love affair with Annette Vallon, told under the disguise of the names Vaudracour and Julia in the 1805 *Prelude*. It is not likely that Wordsworth excluded the affair for aesthetic reasons, though much of it makes rather painful reading. Yet parts of it have a rich, almost passionate tone of excited recollection, and all of it, even as disguised, is crucial for the growth of this poet's soul, little as he seems to have thought so. Nowhere else in his poetry does Wordsworth say of himself, viewing a woman and not Nature, that:

> his present mind
> Was under fascination; he beheld
> A vision, and he lov'd the thing he saw.

Nor does one want to surrender the charm of the prophet of Nature accomplishing a stolen interview at night "with a ladder's help."

Wordsworth was separated from Annette by the war between England and France. In the poem, Vaudracour and Julia are parted by parental opposition. The effects of the parting in life were largely hidden. Wordsworth the man made a happy marriage; Wordsworth the poet did not do as well. Julia goes off to a convent, and Vaudracour goes mad. Either in *The Prelude* or out of it, by presence or by absence, the story is a gap in the poem. Memory curbed was dangerous for Wordsworth; memory falsified was an imaginative fatality.

From the veiled account of his crisis in passion Wordsworth passes, in Books Ten and Eleven, to the crisis in his ideological life, the supreme test of his moral nature. When England went to war against the France of the Revolution, Wordsworth experienced the profound shock of having to exult "when Englishmen by thousands were o'erthrown," and the dark sense:

> Death-like, of treacherous desertion, felt
> In the last place of refuge—my own soul.

The profounder shock of the Terror and of France's career as an external aggressor followed. Wordsworth was adrift, his faith in the Revolution betrayed, and he sought to replace that faith by abstract speculation, and a blind trust in the supreme efficacy of the analytical faculty. He fell, by his own account, into the Ulro of the mechanists and materialists, a rationalism utterly alien to his characteristic modes of thinking and feeling:

> now believing,
> Now disbelieving; endlessly perplexed
> With impulse, motive, right and wrong, the ground
> Of obligation, what the rule and whence
> The sanction; till, demanding formal *proof,*

> And seeking it in every thing, I lost
> All feeling of conviction, and, in fine,
> Sick, wearied out with contrarieties,
> Yielded up moral questions in despair.

Love of Nature had led to love of Man, love of Man to revolutionary hope for Man, and the thwarting of that hope to this unnatural abyss. From these depths the poet's sister was to rescue him, maintaining "a saving intercourse with my true self," as he prays her to do in "Tintern Abbey." In an extraordinary outburst of love for Coleridge, to whom the poem is addressed, the poet invokes a parallel salvation for his friend, to restore him "to health and joy and pure contentedness." He then proceeds, in Books Twelve and Thirteen, to tell of the final stages of his crisis of dejection, the impairment of his Imagination and Taste, and their eventual restoration.

"A bigot to the new idolatry," he:

> Zealously laboured to cut off my heart
> From all the sources of her former strength

The final mark of his fall is to begin to scan the visible universe with the same analytical view he has applied to the moral world. In the aesthetic contemplation pictured in "Tintern Abbey," we see into the life of things because the eye has learned a wise passivity. It has been made quiet by the power of harmony, and the deep power of joy. Bereft of these powers, the poet in his crisis yields to the tyranny of the eye:

> I speak in recollection of a time
> When the bodily eye, in every stage of life
> The most despotic of our senses, gained
> Such strength in *me* as often held my mind
> In absolute dominion.

This fear of visual appearance is at one with Wordsworth's worship of the outward world, though it presents itself as paradox. For the visual surfaces of natural reality are mutable, and Wordsworth desperately quests for a natural reality that can never pass away. That reality, for him, lies just within natural appearance, and the eye made generously passive by nature's generosity is able to trace the lineaments of that final reality, and indeed "half create" it, as "Tintern

Abbey" says. The eye must share, and not seek to appropriate for its own use, for where there is self-appropriation there can be no reality, no covenant of mutual giving. The apocalyptic sense therefore tends to be hearing, as it is in the "Intimations" ode, or that sense of organic fusion, seeing-hearing, which Wordsworth attributes to the infant in that poem. Hartman usefully sums this up as "a vision in which the mind knows itself almost without exterior cause or else as no less real, here, no less indestructible than the object of its perception."

Two agents rescue Wordsworth from the tyranny of the bodily eye, and the consequent impairment of his imagination. One, already spoken of, is Dorothy. The other is the creative doctrine or myth that the poet calls "spots of time":

> There are in our existence spots of time,
> That with distinct pre-eminence retain
> A renovating virtue, whence...
>   ... our minds
> Are nourished and invisibly repaired

This virtue lurks in those episodes of life which tell us precisely how and to what point the individual mind is master of reality, with outward sense merely the mind's servant. Wordsworth gives two incidents as examples, both from his own childhood, as we would expect. In the first he is learning to ride, in the hills, encouraged and guided by his father's servant. Separated by mischance, he dismounts in fear, and leads his horse down the rough and stony moor. He stumbles on a bottom, where once a murderer had hung on a gibbet. Most evidences of an execution place are gone, but local superstition continually clears away the grass, and marks the murderer's name in monumental characters upon the turf. The boy sees them and flees, faltering and faint, losing the road:

> Then, reascending the bare common, saw
> A naked pool that lay beneath the hills,
> The beacon on the summit, and, more near,
> A girl, who bore a pitcher on her head,
> And seemed with difficult steps to force her way
> Against the blowing wind. It was, in truth,
> An ordinary sight; but I should need
> Colours and words that are unknown to man,

> To paint the visionary dreariness
> Which, while I looked all round for my lost guide,
> Invested moorland waste and naked pool,
> The beacon crowning the lone eminence,
> The female and her garments vexed and tossed
> By the strong wind.

The boy's fear of the fresh characters in the turf, and of the moldered gibbet mast, is "natural," as we would say, in these circumstances. But the "visionary dreariness" is a more complex sensation. The common is bare, the pool naked beneath the hills, as open to the eye of heaven as is the pool by which Wordsworth will encounter the Leech Gatherer in "Resolution and Independence," a poem built around a "spot of time." The girl bearing the pitcher struggles against the wind, as winds thwarted winds in the apocalyptic passage in Book Six. Everything that the boy beholds, waste moorland and naked pool, the solitary beacon on the lone eminence, the girl and her garments buffeted by the wind, is similarly dreary, but the nudity and vulnerability of these phenomena, their receptivity to the unchecked power of Nature, unite them in a unified imaginative vision. They blend into one another and into the power to which they offer themselves.

The boy finds no consolation in the scene of visionary dreariness at the time he views it, but he retains it in his memory. Later he returns to the same scene, in the happy hours of early love, his beloved at his side. Upon the scene there falls the gleam of Imagination, with radiance more sublime for the *power* these remembrances had left behind:

> So feeling comes in aid
> Of feeling, and diversity of strength
> Attends us, if but once we have been strong.

The soul, remembering *how* it felt, but what it felt remembering not, has retained the power of a sense of possible sublimity. Imagination, working through memory, appropriates the visionary power and purges the dreariness originally attached to it in this instance. The power is therefore an intimation of the indestructible, for it has survived both initial natural dreariness and the passage of time.

The power is indestructible, but can the poet retain it? We hear again the desperate forebodings of loss:

> The days gone by
> Return upon me almost from the dawn
> Of life: the hiding-places of man's power
> Open; I would approach them, but they close.
> I see by glimpses now; when age comes on,
> May scarcely see at all

The function of the spots of time is to enshrine the spirit of the Past for future restoration. They are meant to be memorials in a lively sense, giving substance and life to what the poet can still feel. That they become memorials in the sepulchral sense also is a sadly unintentional irony.

The poet gives a second example of a spot of time, more complex than the first. Away from home with his brothers, he goes forth into the fields, impatient to see the led palfreys that will bear him back to his father's house. He goes to the summit of a crag over-looking both roads on which the palfreys can come:

> 'twas a day
> Tempestuous, dark, and wild, and on the grass
> I sate half-sheltered by a naked wall;
> Upon my right hand couched a single sheep,
> Upon my left a blasted hawthorn stood

With these companions he watches, as the mist gives intermitting prospect of the plain beneath. Just after this episode, his father dies, and he thinks back to his vigil, with its anxiety of hope:

> And afterwards, the wind and sleety rain,
> And all the business of the elements,
> The single sheep, and the one blasted tree,
> And the bleak music from that old stone wall,
> The noise of wood and water, and the mist
> That on the line of each of those two roads
> Advanced in such indisputable shapes;
> All these were kindred spectacles and sounds
> To which I oft repaired, and thence would drink,
> As at a fountain

What does he drink there? We recognize first in this episode the characteristic quality of the nakedness of the natural scene. The boy is only half sheltered by the naked wall. Beside him, seeking this exposed shelter from the wind, is a single sheep, and on the other side a hawthorn, blasted by the elements. The mist rises all about, blending the landscape into a unity. What can be drunk from this fountain of vulnerable natural identity is, as before, the consciousness of immutable existence, of a life in Nature and in Man which cannot die. This one life within us and abroad must bear the weather, however tempestuous, dark, and wild, but it will not be destroyed if it holds itself open to the elements in loving trust.

Thus "moderated" and "composed" by the spots of time, his faith in Nature restored, the poet is able to say in triumph:

> I found
> Once more in Man an object of delight,
> Of pure imagination, and of love

He is prepared now for his poem's apocalyptic conclusion, the ascent of Mount Snowdon and the vision vouchsafed him there, in Book Fourteen. The poem's structure comes to rest on a point of epiphany, located on a mountain top and associated with the moon and all the mutable world below it, but also with the immutable world above. Girt round by the mist of rising Imagination, the poet looks up to see the Moon hung naked in the azure firmament. The mist stretches in solid vapors, a still ocean as far as the eye can see. In the midst of this ocean, a rift appears, and through the gap:

> Mounted the roar of waters, torrents, streams
> Innumerable, roaring with one voice!
> Heard over earth and sea, and, in that hour,
> For so it seemed, felt by the starry heavens.

The mist, which has for so long figured as an emblem of Imagination in Wordsworth's poetry, now moves to an identity with the emblem of apocalypse, the gathering waters of judgment. The voice of mighty waters makes its strength felt past the point of epiphany, and momentarily influences even the starry heavens. Of this vision the poet says:

> it appeared to me the type
> Of a majestic intellect, its acts
> And its possessions, what it has and craves,
> What in itself it is, and would become.
> There I beheld the emblem of a mind

> That feeds upon infinity, that broods
> Over the dark abyss, intent to hear
> Its voices issuing forth to silent light
> In one continuous stream; a mind sustained
> By recognitions of transcendent power

The whole scene before him is the "type of a majestic intellect," while the moon is the emblem of a mind brooding over the dark abyss. The moon, governing all that is mutable beneath it, feeds upon the infinity of the larger vision to gain an intimation of what is beyond mutability. The moon is like the poet's aroused consciousness, looking up to the indestructible heavens and down at the sea of mist which intimates both the impermanence of the world as we know it (the hint is that it will be flooded again) and its final endurance, after the judgment of the waters. Caught at what Eliot calls "the still point of the turning world," Wordsworth attains to an apprehension of the relation between his moonlike consciousness and the majestic intellect, which now feels the human mind's reciprocal force but which transcends both the human and the natural. What Wordsworth is giving us here is his vision of God, akin to Dante's tremendous vision at the close of the *Paradiso*, except that the mode of this manifestation is still extraordinarily naturalistic. Though not Nature but the power that moves her is revealed, the power's showing forth is not miracle but rather intensification of natural process and visual appearance. Later, in *The Excursion*, Wordsworth will not trust the powers of poetry enough to make so autonomous a statement, to see so human a vision. Here, as he gathers *The Prelude*'s many currents together, he shows a confidence both in his art and in his personal myth of natural salvation. In this confidence he has created a major poem that refreshes life, that is, as Wallace Stevens wrote:

> An elixir, an excitation, a pure power.
> The poem, through candor, brings back a power again
> That gives a candid kind to everything.

Sense in *The Prelude*

William Empson

One does not think of the poetry of Wordsworth, even the parts which expound his philosophy, as depending on a concentrated richness of single words. There are of course "key" words like Nature and Imagination, and these may in reality be very puzzling, but he seems to be making a sturdy effort to expound them in discursive language. The apparently flat little word *sense* has I think a more curious part to play. It comes into practically all the great passages of "Tintern Abbey" and *The Prelude* on the mind's relation to Nature. And so far from being expounded it might seem a kind of expletive that he associates with this line of thought, or a convenience of grammar for expressing it. Yet in fact, of course, whether or not Wordsworth is drawing on Hartley or Coleridge, his whole position depends on some rather undeveloped theory about how the mind interprets what it gets from the senses. Nor does the word drop from him casually; in the great majority of uses he makes it prominent by putting it at the end of the line, and this tends to hold it slightly apart from the stock phrase it comes in, so that some wider meaning for it can be suggested.

Taking Mr. de Selincourt's edition for the 1805 manuscript, I found thirty-five uses of *sense* at the end of a line and twelve elsewhere; the (posthumous) 1850 text has thirty-one uses at the end of a line and eleven elsewhere. There are changes moving the word in

From *The Structure of Complex Words.* © 1951, 1952, 1977 by William Empson. Chatto & Windus and Harvard University Press, 1977.

both directions, but both texts put just under three-quarters of the uses of *sense* at the end of a line, and these I think include all the important uses. The figures are minimal, because no doubt I missed some. I did not count any of the derivative words, even *senseless*. "Tintern Abbey" only uses the word three times, and makes "feeling" do much of the work; but the crucial stylistic inventions for Wordsworth's *sense* come in those three.

The most frequent version of it, as one might expect, is the form "a sense of . . ." which the New English Dictionary explains as "not by direct perception but more or less vaguely or instinctively." This was not a hundred years old, perhaps a good deal less. I shall quote a series of examples with *sense* at the end of the line to show how the effect adds up. [References to *The Prelude* are to the 1850 version unless otherwise noted.] The most famous example, from "Tintern Abbey," has not yet got used to the position for *sense* but gets the corresponding *of* at the start of the next line.

> A sense sublime
> Of something far more deeply interfused
> ("Tintern Abbey," 95)

> While here I stand, not only with the sense
> Of present pleasure, but with pleasing thoughts
> That in this moment there is life and food
> For future years.
> ("Tintern Abbey," 62)

For the surface meaning, *sense* is dragged in here very unnecessarily.

> my brain
> Worked with a dim and undetermined sense
> Of unknown modes of being.
> (Prelude i.391)

There is a suggestion here from the pause at the end of the line that he had not merely "a feeling of" these unknown modes but something like a new "sense" which was partly able to apprehend them—a new *kind* of sensing had appeared in his mind.

> [the soul] retains an obscure sense
> Of possible sublimity
>
> (ii.317)

> Place also by the side of this dark sense
> Of noble feeling, that those spiritual men
> Even the great Newton's own ethereal self,
> Seemed humbled in these precincts thence to be
> The more endeared.
>
> (iii.268)

He is trying to do his best for Cambridge and give it *sense* at the end of a line; but the language is thin, indeed to put his *sense* and *feeling* together always acts as a dilution. But presumably it means "Wordsworth's sense that *they* had noble feelings," so that it would again imply a peculiar mode of knowledge. Most of the later examples of the form are comparatively trivial.

> And though an aching and a barren sense
> Of gay confusion still be uppermost
>
> (iii.627)

> How arch his notices, how nice his sense
> Of the ridiculous
>
> (v.310)

> This only let me add
> From heart-experience, and in humblest sense
> Of modesty
>
> (v.584)

> [from astronomy] I drew
> A pleasure quiet and profound, a sense
> Of permanent and universal sway
>
> (vi.129)

> a sense
> Of what in the Great City had been done
>
> (viii.625)

> When every day brought with it some new sense
> Of exquisite regard for common things.
>
> (xiv.262)

And, to end with something more worth attention,

> a voice
> Labouring, a brain confounded, and a sense,
> Death-like, of treacherous desertion, felt
> In that last place of refuge, my own soul.
>
> (x.412)

I only noticed five cases where "a sense of" is used without *sense* being at the end of a line. They come fairly late in the poem and carry none of this weight (e.g. "sense of beauty" viii.74, "of right" ix.388).

The word, of course, can also be used merely for one of the senses:

> As we grow up, such thraldom of that sense
> Seems hard to shun.
>
> (xii.150)

Here it is the sense of sight, or rather the pleasure in scenery, which tends to have too much power. The word is simple enough, but even here he is not merely thinking of reception of sense data.

Also, examples of *sense* meaning only "good judgment" or "common sense" undoubtedly occur:

> that were to lack
> All sense . . .
>
> (iii.367)

> To tell us what is passion, what is truth,
> What reason, what simplicity and sense.
>
> (vi.113)

> Words follow words, sense seems to follow sense.
>
> (vii.507)

In one place we even have a bad kind of *sense*:

> The tendency, too potent in itself,
> Of use and custom to bow down the soul
> Under a growing weight of vulgar sense
> (xiv.157)

"Oppress it by the laws of vulgar sense" is the 1805 version. The idea I suppose is "what vulgar people call good sense, knowing the price of things, etc." It comes very late in the poem. In any case, all these are in a way negative uses; in the positive ones he makes "good sense" something larger than the ordinary idea of it. Even

> real feeling and just sense
> (xiii.172)

has a peculiar emphasis. In spite of his disadvantages, he reflects, he might have had a good effect on the French Revolution if he had tried, because any man might

> That with desires heroic and firm sense
> (x.166, 1805)

had made a bold stand. In the 1850 version, this has become "strong in hope, and trained to noble aspirations"; Wordsworth perhaps felt that the reader could not be expected to know how much he had felt *sense* to imply. Even the phrase "common sense" makes an appearance in the 1805 version, but certainly looks bigger than usual. It is about the unfortunate child who has been educated from books:

> Forth bring him to the light of common sense
> And, fresh and shewy as he is, the Corpse
> Slips from us into powder.
> (v.354, 1805)

While cutting this out of the 1850 version, Wordsworth put back "common sense" a little higher up, in a flat appeal to the reader which feels rather out of the style. In any case, though the idea "common sense" occurs, an adjective will often be added to this version of *sense* to make it carry higher claims:

> one whom circumstance
> Hath called upon to embody his deep sense
> In action, give it outwardly a shape,
> And that of benediction, to the world.
> (ix.400)

Good judgment here becomes practically the Creative Imagination applied to politics.

> He deemed that my pursuits and labours lay
> Apart from all that leads to wealth, or even
> A necessary maintenance insures,
> Without some hazard to the finer sense.
>
> (xiv. 364)

This rather pompous stuff is almost exactly the prosaic use of "sensibility"; it is viewed as a special degree of "good judgment" but hints vaguely at something more artistic. The passage is the same in the 1805 version.

I think it is important that Wordsworth refuses to say "sensibility" in these poems at all, except once about babies (ii.270) and once about the growing child who still has some of the claims of the baby (ii.360). Babies are entitled to a "tender, delicate, easily hurt" kind of sensibility, what "The Man of Feeling" had been proud of, but not (in Wordsworth's view) adults. Excessive sensibility was, I suppose, connected in his mind with the modish affectations of the people who used Poetic Diction, and he would not have liked his contemporary Marianne Dashwood, but to make a direct attack on the word might have been confusing. Cutting it out had an unexpected but rather helpful consequence; it put a lot of extra work on *sense* and thereby made the word more fluid.

There are points, indeed, where the language tells us plainly that a new kind of *sense* is in question. To begin with a slighter case, he suggests that poets

> Have each for his peculiar dower, a sense
> By which he is enabled to perceive
> Something unseen before
>
> (xiii.304, 1805)

and perhaps this will show Wordsworth what used to happen at Stonehenge. The 1850 edition reduces the suggestion of vanity in this fancy by removing *sense* from the end of the line. Again we have:

> Nor less do I remember to have felt
> Distinctly manifested at this time
> A dawning, even as of another sense,

> A human-heartedness about my love
> For objects hitherto the gladsome air
> Of my own private being and no more.
>   (iv.222, 1805)

This seems to throw light on a use of the word twenty lines earlier:

> Yes, I had something of another eye
> And looking round was often moved to smiles
> Such as a delicate work of humour breeds.
> I read, without design, the opinions, thoughts
> Of these plainliving people, in a sense
> Of love and knowledge.
>   (iv.200, 1805)

Such is the 1805 version; [I give the line reference to the 1850 one for convenience.] There it is altered to "now observed with clearer knowledge." Wordsworth, no doubt, felt that this use of *sense* would hardly be intelligible, and indeed it must mean that he read them with a new faculty of sensing. Unfortunately, he chose to get his pet word back into the text somehow, and it comes in the first line of the paragraph, very intelligibly, but with a disagreeable complacence:

> Yes, I had something of a subtler sense.
>   (iv.209, 1850)

The passage about the Chartreuse, which was entirely rewritten, gives a more striking example of how he came to alter his idea of the word:

> be the house redeemed
> With its unworldly votaries, for the sake
> Of conquest over sense, hourly achieved
> Through faith and meditative reason.
>   (vi.456)

The 1805 version has no example of *sense* meaning sensuality, and this I should think was deliberate. Even for the 1850 one, Wordsworth did not allow it to come at the end of a line. His own "conquest over sense" is something of an unwanted irony here.

More general examples of the same process are given by "The incumbent mystery of sense and soul" (xiv.286, 1850) and "By sense conducting to ideal form" (xiv.76), where he is introducing at least the hint of a dichotomy in the course of re-writing; *sense* appears to be the opposite of soul, and the "mystery" is that they can be connected at all. However, I do not want to make out that the re-writing shows an important change of opinion. In any case, there are signs that his use of the word had changed in the six years between ending Book Six and starting Book Seven; all the impressive examples come before that. What is really in question, I think, is not any theory in Wordsworth's mind about the word but a manipulative feeling, of what he could make it do; a thing more familiar perhaps to poets than critics, and one which a poet easily forgets; the period during which Wordsworth could feel how to use this word was, I think, very brief. In general, I agree with a recent defender of the older man (M. E. Burton, *One Wordsworth*) who says that he did not try to hide his early political and religious opinions any further when he re-wrote, indeed, he sometimes enlarged upon a vaguely unorthodox idea such as the world-soul; he was merely "improving the style." But this improvement, which was mainly a process of packing the lines more fully, meant invoking Milton and his sense of the unrelaxing Will; whereas the whole point and delicacy of the first version was to represent a wavering and untrammelled natural growth. The improvement was, therefore, about the most destructive thing he could have done, far worse than changing the supposed opinions. Incidentally, I think there was also a good influence of Milton, already strong in the first version, which came from a very different side of that author's feeling about the world; it is remarkable surely that the first paragraph of *The Prelude*, describing how Wordsworth is now free to wander where he chooses and write as much as he likes, makes two distinct quotations from the throwing out from Paradise of Adam and Eve ("The earth is all before me" (i.14.), "Whither shall I turn?" (i.26)). Indeed the repeated claims that it was somehow a good thing to have lost his first inspiration are a rather close parallel to Milton's baffling but very strong feelings about Paradise.

I have tried to review the general background of the uses, and must now approach the important ones.

> in such strength
> Of usurpation, when the light of sense
> Goes out, but with a flash that has revealed
> The invisible world, doth greatness make abode.
> (vi.599)

Maybe this tidier version of the great passage is an improvement, but the 1805 one certainly demands attention:

> in such strength
> Of usurpation, in such visitings
> Of awful promise, when the light of sense
> Goes out in flashes that have shown to us
> The invisible world, doth greatness make abode.
>
> (vi.532, 1805)

It is not long after the Chartreuse passage, and perhaps Wordsworth in making his changes remembered the ascetic view of *sense* he had put in for the monks. The removal of the sensuous world, in the new version, is the point of vision. But this idea was already present in the old one; the *invisible world* clearly means to suggest something like it. I am rather reluctant to insist on the ambiguity of the passage, because in general the style does not want any concentrated piece of trickery; Wordsworth is trying to state his position, even if he fails. But the trick he has stumbled upon here is as glorious as such a thing could be. *The light . . . goes out* can mean "light proceeds from the source" as well as "the source fails." By combining the two, Wordsworth induces his baffling *sense* to become a lighthouse occasionally flashing not on any spiritual world but on the dangerous and actual sea, which at other times is invisible merely because the captain is in darkness. I am not certain, to be sure, whether lighthouses already flashed in Wordsworth's time, and the essential image is the last bright flash of the guttering candle; this in itself allows mere sensation to carry mysterious and rarely seen powers. The ecstasy both destroys normal *sense* and fulfills it, and the world thus shown is both the same as and wholly different from the common one. The verbal ambiguity in the first version only drives home the paradox which he retained in the later one.

The most fundamental statement of this theory of the senses is made about the famous baby at the breast:

> For him, in one dear Presence, there exists
> A virtue which irradiates and exalts
> Objects through widest intercourse of sense.
> No outcast he, bewildered and depress . . .
> For, feeling has to him imparted power
> That through the growing faculties of sense

> Doth like an agent of the one great Mind
> Create, creator and receiver both,
> Working but in alliance with the works
> Which it beholds.
>
> (ii.238–60)

The 1805 version brings in *sensations* and *sentiment* but does not have *sense* twice:

> In one beloved presence, nay and more
> In that most apprehensive habitude
> And those sensations which have been derived
> From this beloved Presence, there exists
>
> (ii.255, 1805)

"a virtue" and so on, and

> For feeling has to him imparted strength
> And powerful in all sentiments of grief
> Of exultation, fear, and joy, his mind
> Even as an agent of the one great Mind,
>
> (ii.269, 1805)

"creates" and so on. The earlier version is thus rather more pantheist, emphasises emotion more, and is perhaps less dependent on key words; the notion that feeling "returns as power" had come to seem a settled epigram to Wordsworth when he shortened the second part of this quotation, and in the same way it seemed an adequate theoretical coverage to say "faculties of sense" rather than list the child's emotions, which might suggest that he admired it (as the Chinese sage Laotze did) because it yelled so loudly. In the first part of the quotation the change makes the idea prettier and cruder; the original point was that the "sensation" of affection, and I suppose of resistance as well, towards the mother are what teach the "senses" of the child to grasp the world, a thing which must be done by an interchange like that between persons. *Sensations* here are not sense data, and thereby free from the ambiguity of *sense*, but a more highly developed compound of emotion and knowledge even than *sense*, and therefore convenient for forcing us to understand it. Indeed, the 1805 version has no unambiguous term for sense data, and I suppose would have denied the reality of the concept; in the 1850 version Wordsworth sometimes inserts "bodily" before *sense* to make a passage clearer (e.g., xiv.88) but the earlier version hardly ever descends to this (once in 1805 xi.272).

Obviously the meaning "good judgment" is given a very back seat when the word is used for such a theory. It need not be ignored or denied, but it is only a middling part of the range which has now to be covered by the word, and we are more interested in the two ends of the range. Using the word for the baby makes the process more complete. No doubt the baby does have to use good judgment, but its powers of mind are applied to such extraordinary things from our point of view, the building up of the idea of space for example, that we do not think of them as needing "good sense." The whole poetical and philosophical effect comes from a violent junction of sense data to the divine imagination given by love, and the middle term is cut out.

The uses of the word so far, however striking, can be said to keep within its previous range. It appears that Wordsworth also invented a new form, "the sense" used absolutely, and the new form must be supposed to imply some new meaning. There are, to be sure, precedents for the form, but only with a context that makes the meaning an obvious one. The New English Dictionary has "5," "pierced to the sense" (to the quick); "11b," "if they had had the sense to do it they could have . . . "; and "1e," "the process of ink-making is noisome to the sense." Perhaps this last heading, defined as "that one of the senses indicated by the context," would cover Lucio's "wanton stings and motions of the sense," which otherwise seems to be ignored. Pope has a use which feels more like those of Wordsworth, "darkness strikes the sense no less than light," but I take it he meant quite narrowly "the sense of sight." None of these would prevent the bare and blank use by Wordsworth from appearing a novelty. He has already got it in "Tintern Abbey," and it is already tearing upon the tripod:

> well pleased to recognize
> In Nature and the language of the sense,
> The anchor of my purest thoughts, the nurse,
> The guide, the guardian of my heart, and soul
> Of all my moral being.
>
> ("Tintern Abbey," 108)

"The" does not refer back to any *sense* previously defined, but this very sentence is expressing his theory; it goes

> Therefore am I still
> A lover of the meadows and the woods...
> of all the mighty world
> Of eye and ear—both what they half create,
> And what perceive; well pleased to recognize
> ("Tintern Abbey," 102)

Thus one feels that "the sense" is a combination of "that sense" (the kind of *sense* just adumbrated) and "the senses" in general. The new grammar was really needed by the poetry; even Wordsworth could not have got away with saying that the language of *the senses* was the soul of all his moral being. "*Language*" does much of the work— the senses can no doubt "show" us profound things (like Professor Wittgenstein) through the means by which they "tell" us everyday things; but the traditional idea of the weakness and corruptibility of the senses would have been bound to poke up its head. With the new grammar "the sense" can take over some of the defining work from "the language"; we may even take "the sense" as a peculiar power of imagination and its "language" as the mere sense data from which we learn it. Either term could serve to ward off misunderstanding.

After this invention of the form he used it without any help from the context.

> Nor, sedulous as I have been to trace
> How Nature by extrinsic passion first
> Peopled the mind with forms sublime or fair,
> And made me love them, may I here omit
> How other pleasures have been mine, and joys
> Of subtler origin; how I have felt,
> Not seldom even in that tempestuous time,
> Those hallowed and pure motions of the sense
> Which seem, in their simplicity, to own
> An intellectual charm; that calm delight
> Which, if I err not, surely must belong
> To those first-born affinities that fit
> Our new existence to existing things,
> And, in our dawn of being, constitute
> The bond of union between life and joy.

> Yes, I remember when the changeful earth
> And twice five summers on my mind had
>   stamped
> The faces of the moving year, even then
> I held unconscious intercourse with beauty
> Old as creation, drinking in a pure
> Organic pleasure from the silver wreaths
> Of curling mist, or from the level plain
> Of waters coloured by impending clouds.
>   (i.544–66)

The 1805 version is noticeably better in the last five lines, but there is no important difference elsewhere:

> A Child, I held unconscious intercourse
> With the eternal Beauty, drinking in
> A pure organic pleasure from the lines
> Of curling mist, or from the level plain
> Of waters coloured by the steady clouds.
>   (i.589–593, 1805)

The next paragraph says he would stand looking at the water

>   bringing with me no peculiar sense
>   Of quietness or peace
>   (i.603, 1805)

but "gathering . . . New pleasure, like a bee among the flowers."

Wordsworth, I think, realised that he had to use hidden devices so that he might talk as if he had never heard of the meaning "sensuality"; the chief function of *pure* here is to keep it out of view. But apart from this hidden denial of a meaning (a common and important process), which adds obscurity to the uses of the word, there is a curious blankness even about the meanings allowed. I have quoted at length here to show how the context before and after leads us in the two opposite directions. The second sentence, or paragraph, begins by saying that he remembers taking a pure organic pleasure in the scenery at this period (when he was ten). But the beginning of the first long sentence makes a careful distinction between his love for the scenery and the "joys of subtler origin"; and these are what he is claiming to remember. I am not saying that there is a real contradiction in this obscurity, only that it imposes a double meaning on "the sense." If the child were enjoying the scenery we would expect the term to mean or anyway to include "the senses," but our attention is first directed away from them so that it means some "inner sense," and *the* in the singular makes it look like the supreme sense of Imagination. But then the next sentence pushes it back to the sensations about the scenery again. I take it that the child felt a gush of well-being from far within, apparently without cause, but marking some profound adjustment to life; and Wordsworth goes on to say that he remembers attaching this feeling to the scenery. The effect is that, though Sensation and Imagination appear as the two extreme ends of the scale in view, so that one might expect them to be opposites, the word is so placed that it might equally well apply to either. And the middle of the scale, the idea of ordinary common sense, is cut out from these uses no less firmly than the idea of sensuality. That is, instead of falling into the usual fallacies about good sense, you are forced to keep the whole range of the word in view, and there is a claim that the whole range of the word has been included in one concept. At least, I do not see what else the claim can be, and I suppose most people would agree that the word is made to echo Wordsworth's doctrine somehow.

A conceivable meaning for *the sense* is the archaic "common sense," that which correlates the messages of the different external senses. It is "the senses regarded as unified," and that is already a kind of rudimentary power of interpreting them. It was not then so remote as to be unfamiliar to Wordsworth. On the other hand, the passage as a whole obviously means "My Imagination was already stirring," but which of the words means his imagination, if *the sense* does not? This may be an unreasonable process of thought, but it seems to describe the way we are driven to give the term an obscure but splendid claim. It must be remembered that, here as so often in the poem, the language is in any case extremely loose; the theoretical turns of phrase in the first paragraph lead us to expect the "bond of union" to be between the child and the external world—an epistemology is being given—but the peroration sweeps this aside to contemplate only "life and joy." No doubt the reason why this seems fine is that one accepts *life* as the child and *joy* as inherent in Mother Nature, but such extreme optimism is made plausible only by being left vague. In the same way *the sense* feels inherently vague; but this is no reason why we should not try to account for its behaviour.

In the "Statements in Words" chapter I gave as an example of the fourth type the use of *law* for "both human and divine law"; the law you are talking about will commonly appear to be one or the other, but you may imply that such laws as this one satisfy the conditions for both. In such a case, though the order of terms for the equation is indifferent, it will be fixed on any particular occasion. The Wordsworthian use of *sense*, if I am right, is a much more thorough example of the process, not merely because the unifying concept required is much more obscure, but because in any one use of the equation you are not certain which term is meant to come first. However, I should claim that these two sorts of equation can be classed together for the purpose in hand, which is to consider what the different forms of interpretation can be.

Granting that the Wordsworth one is an equation of some sort, it is still not obvious how this equation could be translated into a sentence. "Sensation is Imagination" is a possible slogan, but both this and its inverse seem very open to misunderstanding without making the real point. "Sensation and Imagination are included in a larger class" is merely dull; besides, the important thing may well be that they overlap to form a narrower class. "Sensation and Imagination interlock" seems the best way to put it. But I think it is fair to say that Wordsworth had not got any translation ready; he was much better at adumbrating his doctrine through rhetorical devices than at writing it out in full.

To be sure, I do not mean to claim that the form always carries so much weight; for example it is used in the 1805 version to build a graceful piece of deliberate tedium, later omitted.

> On I went
> Tranquil, receiving in my own despite
> Amusement, as I slowly passed along,
> From such near objects as from time to time
> Perforce, intruded on the listless sense,
> Quiescent, and disposed for sympathy.
> (iv.375, 1805)

Even here it can be read as something like "imagination"; indeed, you might say that Wordsworth, rather pompously, is thinking of his imagination as a pet dog which never left his side. The example shows that the form was still connected in his mind with the actual process of receiving sensations. But, in contrast to that, another of these fairly trivial uses shows him treating it as a sort of technical term. During the French Revolution, he is saying, many young idealists and theorists felt that they must learn to deal with practical affairs:

> The playfellows of fancy, who had made
> All powers of swiftness, subtlety, and strength
> Their ministers, who in lordly wise had stirred
> Among the grandest objects of the sense,
> And dealth with whatsoever they found there
> As if they had within some lurking right
> To wield it . . .
> Were called upon to exercise their skill
>
> (xi.126)

—in the real world. This is particularly baffling because *the sense* appears to be the despised Fancy. In ordinary English, that is, you would expect it to refer to a sense *of* a kind already mentioned, and a sense of fancy is the only plausible candidate. But it is considered ironical that these people thought they had a right to deal with whatever they *found there*, that is, in *the sense* or among its *grandest objects*. Of course, it may be said that fancy often deals with grand objects, only not practically enough. The irony of Wordsworth is always cumbrous, and he does not mean to express contempt for these people by it (the passage is hardly altered from 1805); nor therefore, you might argue, for their kind of fancy. I do not see how to disprove such an argument, but I believe that at this stage of the poem he regarded *the sense* as practically equivalent to "Imagination," so that it comes in as a natural opposite to Fancy (the irony against these people is due because they supposed that fancy would work where imagination is required). I think, indeed, that he would have been startled to find anyone identifying the two opposites for reasons of grammar. The interest of the example, supposing that this account is true, is that he was taking his new form as something well established.

I ought now to give some account of *feeling*. One might think that it was the opposite word to *sense*, rather as *wit* is in Pope, but Wordsworth does not oppose the two words, and the effect when he puts them together is one of verbosity rather than anything else. Both of them (and *sensation* too) are concerned with both knowledge and emotion; a feeling of impending doom is very like a sense of one. The choice between using one or the other is I think often made on rather obscure grounds of tact. "A sense of" impending doom claims that there is really something there to feel, though your interpretation of it may be wrong, whereas "a feeling of it" admits that you may be wholly mistaken. However, this contrast may be used in a rather contradictory way. If you want to say that you have come to a decision, though you realise the subject is complicated, you say you "feel," and whatever the other man says you can still have your feeling. To say you have a *sense* that your plan is the best would really be milder, though it makes a larger claim, because it is not wholly closed to argument. "When people begin to 'feel'," Samuel Butler noticed, "they are always taking what seems to them the more worldly course." It is because the subject is so complicated (not a thing you could claim to know about) that they are prepared to act in a way which might seem against their principles. This rather odd social development makes it hard to nail down a difference between the words in general. I should fancy that Wordsworth made more use of *feeling* in "Tintern Abbey" because he was writing with more direct conviction, though no doubt it is also true that he had not yet fixed his technical terms. But in any case it does not seem possible to exchange the words in his later work:

> So feeling comes in aid
> Of feeling, and diversity of strength
> Attends us, if but once we have been strong.
> (xii.269)

The whole passage is a very fine one. But why could not Wordsworth use his technical terms here?

> A single operation of the sense
> Gives power, and diversity of strength

Why, I wonder, does my invention look so ridiculous? No doubt it fails to meet the point about "diversity"; it seems a narrow piece of theorising. But also I think it feels out of the style because it makes *the sense* too definite; only some high idea of "the sense of imagination" will fit the requirements of the assertion, whereas Wordsworth always (even in "the grandest objects of the sense") left room for the alternative reading by which it meant the processes of sensing in general. Indeed, this double meaning was required by the theory which he used it to expound.

The reader may also have felt my little attempt ridiculous because he remembered the context, which is a particularly strange one. "I am lost," Wordsworth is just going to say; he uses *feeling* for a reason not really unlike that of Samuel Butler's people, and in any case he is actually talking about feelings rather than some act of imagination which would transcend them. He first describes the fear of the child losing its guide on the grim moor, and the "visionary dreariness" of the place, and then says that this place, when he came back "in the blessed hours / Of early love, the loved one at my side," gave him ideas of "pleasure and youth's golden gleam."

> And think ye not with radiance more sublime
> For these remembrances, and for the power
> They had left behind? So feeling comes in aid
> (xii.267)

It is not even clear that the child used *the sense*; the only strength he showed was to face and recognise the horror of the thing. And what kind of strength does Wordsworth now require, out walking with the bride rather coldly planned for? Apparently even a time of agony in his childhood was better than—more than that, it gave him strength to endure—the chief pleasure he could arrange for his middle age. Of course, he would have denied that he had meant this, but he is reporting experiences, without much distortion for the sake of theory, and it would be no use to try to simplify his opinions.

Mr. James Smith has pointed out a similar jump in the famous passage on crossing the Alps, and it has the advantage for my purpose of falling into an "A is B" form. Critics have insinuated that the experience was a good deal "written up," judging by Wordsworth's travel diary, but if you examine the language of the poem it is sufficiently frank. On being told that he had crossed the Alps, he says, "Imagination"—

> That awful Power rose from the mind's abyss
> Like an unfathered vapour that enwraps,
> At once, some lonely traveller. I was lost;
> Halted without an effort to break through;
> But to my conscious soul I now can say
> "I recognise thy glory"; in such strength
> Of usurpation
> (vi.594)

—and "the light of sense goes out." The 1850 version says rather more clearly than the 1805 one ("and now recovering, to my soul I say") that he only recognised the Imagination afterwards, but they both say it. The next paragraph, indeed, calmly begins by saying that what this news caused at the time was "a melancholy slackening." But they hurry on down the gorge and see

> The immeasurable height
> Of woods decaying, never to be decayed...
> Winds thwarting winds, bewildered and forlorn...
> The rocks that muttered close upon our ears,
> Black drizzling crags that spake by the way-side
> As if a voice were in them; the sick sight
> And giddy prospect of the raving stream
> (vi.624–633)

Nature is a ghastly threat in this fine description; he might well, as in his childhood, have clasped a tree to see if it was real. But what all this is *like*, when the long sentence arrives at its peroration, is "workings of one mind," (presumably God's or Nature's, so it is not merely *like*)

> Characters of the great Apocalypse,
> The types and symbols of Eternity,
> Of first, and last, and midst, and without end.
> (vi.638)

The actual horror and the eventual exultation are quite blankly identified by this form of grammar. Now, of course, the historical process of learning to enjoy mountains really was a matter of taking this jump. I do not want to appear more prosy than Jane Austen on the subject. Her chief discussion of it comes in *Sense and Sensibility*, Chapter Eighteen, and we find she is perfectly at home with horror; the man who says he likes scenery to be cheerful is suspected of trying to be singular, but on the whole, it is felt, he is only rebuking excess or sympathising with farmers—at bottom he likes horror all right, like any other person of taste. One need not say, as I understand Mr. James Smith to do, that owing to a narrow theory about Nature Wordsworth is forcing an obviously wrong interpretation onto his feelings here. The point of identifying these two very different states of feeling, as a matter of style, is to insist that they are profoundly connected; one of them grows out of the other, or something like that. No doubt some kind of pantheism is implied, because Wordsworth feels that Eternity is turbulent like the Alps and not calm like the Christian God. But the last line of the passage contradicts this idea by putting the calm back, and in any case the metaphysics would be a deduction only; what he sets out to do is to describe the whole development of his feelings about crossing the Alps, and he asserts it as a unity.

I have been wandering away here from the verbal approach and the word *sense*, and I needed to do so, because if my account of *sense* is to be convincing I need to show that a similar process is at work generally in the poem. The word, I maintain, means both the process of sensing and the supreme act of imagination, and unites them by a jump; the same kind of jump as that in the sentence about crossing the Alps, which identifies the horror caused by the immediate sensations with the exultation that developed from them. And in both cases, one might complain, what is jumped over is "good sense"; when Wordsworth has got his singing robes on he will not allow any mediating process to have occurred.

A sturdy Wordsworthian, I suppose, would answer that there really is a consistent theory expounded, and that my linguistic approach merely ignores it. But then the Hartley theory, which Mr. Herbert Read describes as "practically what would now be called Behaviourism," left much the same gap to be jumped. Perhaps I should quote some of his exposition of it (in his *Wordsworth*):

> According to Hartley's psychology, our passions or affections are no more than aggregates of simple ideas united by association, and simple ideas are ideas surviving sensations after the objects which caused them have been removed. First, sensations, which arise from the impressions made by external objects upon the different parts of our bodies; then simple ideas of sensation; finally, under the power of association, all the various faculties of the human mind, such as memory, imagination, understanding, affection, and will.

Indeed, there is at least one passage, in the rejected manuscript Y given in Mr de Selincourt's edition, where Wordsworth positively asserts the connection of ideas which I claim to find buried in his use of *the sense*. After the child has grasped simple ideas, he says:

> And the world's native produce, as it meets
> The sense with less habitual strength of mind,
> Is pondered as a miracle,

he grows up wanting to believe myths and legends; but the wiser man after maturity will abandon them and return to the Nature which the child experienced,

> as it were
> Resolving into one great faculty
> Of being bodily eye and spiritual need

and there is a very fine long passage about the strength which his thought can then attain. There is no unwillingness to expound the idea in this rejected and rather bold document; we are plainly told that the new faculty combines sensation and imagination. Perhaps I am taking a narrow and stupid view, but the idea seems to me to remain pretty unintelligible, however plainly and lengthily it is expressed, and at any rate most readers of the poetry, who have not read Hartley, must pick up the idea in the form which I have tried to describe. Besides, Wordsworth seems to have followed Coleridge in going to the opposite philosophical extreme, from Associationism to Idealism, without feeling that the change needed to be made obvious in these poetical expressions of his theory. It does not seem unfair to say that he induced people to believe he had expounded a consistent philosophy through the firmness and assurance with which he used equations of Type IV; equations whose claim was false, because they did not really erect a third concept as they pretended to; and in saying this I do not mean to deny that the result makes very good poetry, and probably suggests important truths.

Syntax in the Blank Verse of Wordsworth's *Prelude*

Donald Davie

We have to understand that when St.-John Perse speaks of the Englishman as enamoured of "nature," he means the "nature" of Isaac Newton. If the clue to Newton had not been given, we might have gone astray. We might have thought first of Wordsworth. For it is Wordsworth who springs most readily to mind as the sort of English poet that the Frenchman finds alien, the poet "enamoured of nature" and "rediscovering (his) infinite in the cosmic abyss." But the abyss, we now realize, is not what evoked in Wordsworth "fleeting moods of shadowy exultation"; what the French poet means is "a world of atoms in motion, devoid of all secondary sense qualities, such as colour, scent, taste and sound, ordered by causal laws and explicable only in terms of mathematics"—in short, the world of abstract "matter" in which the early experimenters seemed to find themselves, when they followed out the implications of their conscientiously "concrete" experiments.

Far from making against Wordsworth, Perse's view of poetic language, I shall suggest, is the one best fitted to account for some of Wordsworth's verse. Only in terms of words as "fiduciary symbols" can Wordsworth's blank verse in *The Prelude* be properly appreciated. In those passages of *The Prelude* where Wordsworth is trying to convey most exactly the effect of the natural world upon himself, his words ("ties" and "bonds" and "influences" and "pow-

From *Articulate Energy: An Inquiry into the Syntax of English Poetry.* © 1955 by Donald Davie. First American edition, Harcourt, Brace & Co., 1958.

ers") will carry the reader only (as Valéry says) so long as he does not loiter, so long as they are taken, as coins are taken, "as values of monetary exchange." Wordsworth's words have meaning so long as we trust them. They have just such meaning, and just as much meaning, as Perse and Valéry suggest.

We can make a start by pointing out that Wordsworth's world is not preeminently a world of "things." His language has not, in St.-John Perse's sense, "weight and mass." It is not concrete. Because in the Preface to *Lyrical Ballads* Wordsworth castigated some earlier poets for giving no proof that they had ever truly *looked* at natural phenomena, it is often supposed that his own verse is full of such phenomena rendered in all their quiddity and concreteness. But this is a sort of optical illusion. What Wordsworth renders is not the natural world but (with masterly fidelity) the effect that world has upon him. He is at all points a very long way from "trying to reincarnate the thing itself, as in ideographic writing." As Lionel Trilling remarks (in *The Liberal Imagination*):

> Wordsworth never did have the special and perhaps modern sensibility of his sister or of Coleridge, who were so aware of exquisite particularities. His finest passages are moral, emotional, subjective; whatever visual intensity they have comes from his response to the object, not from his close observation of it.

On the contrary, I have heard more than one student complain of Wordsworth's diction that it is too "abstract." I shall argue that the diction of *The Prelude* is neither abstract nor concrete, but something between the two.

This gives me the chance to introduce a very weighty objection to Ernest Fenollosa's theory of poetic language. It will be remembered that according to him, "At the base of the pyramid lie *things*, but stunned, as it were." T.C. Pollock, however, sees in this view the fallacy of "Misplaced Concreteness":

> If an abstract term is the sign of an abstraction from an individual experience (E) or a group of individual experiences (E), a non-abstract or a concrete term would be the sign of that from which the abstraction was drawn, the non-abstract individual experience (E) or the non-abstract individual experiences (E) in the group of experiences

(E). The opposite of an abstract term would therefore be, not the name of a specific or "concrete" object, but the sign of a total or concrete *experience* (E). The error arises because of the assumption that the abstraction is from *objects*, instead of from *experiences* (E). (On the contrary, what we call "objects" are psychologically abstractions from *experiences* (E).)

As Pollock goes on to show (in *The Nature of Literature*), this statement is only the counterpart in linguistic theory of a fact of linguistic history, the fact established by Jespersen that originally words stood for whole *experiences*, which were only subsequently broken down into "seen" things and "unseen" feelings about them, or significances in them. Fenollosa's account of metaphor is at odds with Jespersen, as his account of abstraction is at odds with Pollock.

Now if Wordsworth was concerned to render his responses to the natural world, he was concerned with experiences, and these were "concretions" from which he did not care to abstract (as his sister and Coleridge did) that part of them which we call "objects" or "things." It follows that ideographic writing, in which words embody things, is *more abstract than* writing in which words are fiduciary symbols for elements of an experience.

This view of words as symbols is advanced by Coleridge in a famous passage from *Biographia Literaria*:

> The best part of human language, properly so called, is derived from reflection on the acts of the mind itself. It is formed by a voluntary appropriation of fixed symbols to internal acts, to processes and results of imagination, the greater part of which have no place in the consciousness of uneducated man; though in civilized society, by imitation and passive remembrance of what they hear from their religious instructors and other superiors, the most uneducated share in the harvest which they neither sowed nor reaped.

It will be recalled that this statement is made when Coleridge is objecting to Wordsworth's recommendation of rustic language, on the grounds that such language can provide only poor and meagre syntax:

> The rustic, from the more imperfect development of his faculties, and from the lower state of their cultivation, aims almost solely to convey insulated facts, either those of his scanty experience or his traditional belief; while the educated man chiefly seeks to discover and express those connections of things, or those relative bearings of fact to fact, from which some more or less general law is deducible. For facts are valuable to a wise man, chiefly as they lead to the discovery of the indwelling law, which is the true being of things, the sole solution of their modes of existence, and in the knowledge of which consists our dignity and our power.

Coleridge points out, what Perse and Valéry have led us to expect, that if a language is deficient in "fixed symbols" for "internal acts," it will also be deficient in syntax. I shall proceed to show that Wordsworth, when he abandoned rustic diction and took to rendering "internal acts," "processes and results of imagination," used for the purpose an elaborate syntax, and that an important part of his vocabulary is neither abstract nor concrete, but made up of fixed fiduciary symbols.

In *The Prelude* the syntax is elaborately correct:

> I deem not profitless these fleeting moods
> Of shadowy exultation: not for this,
> That they are kindred to our purer mind
> And intellectual life; but that the soul,
> Remembering how she felt, but what she felt
> Remembering not, retains an obscure sense
> Of possible sublimity, to which
> With growing faculties she doth aspire,
> With faculties still growing, feeling still
> That whatsoever point they gain, they still
> Have something to pursue.

Dr. Leavis comments on this passage (in *Revaluation*):

> It would be difficult to suggest anything more elusive than this possibility which the soul glimpses in "visionary" moments and,
>
>> "Remembering how she felt, but what she felt
>> Remembering not,"

retains an "obscure sense" of. Perhaps it will be agreed that, though Wordsworth no doubt was right in feeling that he had something to pursue, the critic here is in a different case. If these "moments" have any significance for the critic (whose business it is to define the significance of Wordsworth's poetry), it will be established, not by dwelling upon or in them, in the hope of exploring something that lies hidden in or behind their vagueness, but by holding firmly on to that sober verse in which they are presented.

I may be misreading Dr. Leavis, but it seems to me that what is recommended here is what Perse and Valéry recommend: taking the verse at a run, not pausing on the nouns for fear they congeal into the staring unfathomable eyes that appalled Hofmannsthal, but attending rather to the syntactical weave. If this is what Dr. Leavis means, the testimony is all the more valuable as coming from a reader who in other cases (on Milton, for instance, as we have seen) is cautious not to grant the poet all that he asks for. What Wordsworth asks for here is for all his words to be considered only in their context. Yet it is different from what Pound asks for in the *Cantos*. These moods, exultations, senses, sublimities, and faculties will be no clearer at the end of *The Prelude* than they are here; and yet the poem will not be a botch, for what will be clear at the end is the relationship between them, the articulation. The nouns are not concrete; but the verbs are, and may be lingered over. In short, this is poetry where the syntax counts enormously, counts for nearly everything.

Earlier, however . . . Dr. Leavis has remarked of this blank verse:

Wordsworth in such passages as are in question produces the mood, feeling or experience and at the same time appears to be giving an explanation of it. The expository effect sorts well with—blends into—the characteristic meditative gravity of the emotional presentment ("emotion recollected in tranquillity"), and in the key passages, where significance seems specially to reside, the convincing success of the poetry covers the argument: it is only by the most resolute and sustained effort (once it occurs to one that effort is needed) that one can pay to the argument, as such, the attention it appears to have invited and satisfied.

And Dr. Leavis directs us to William Empson to see how ill the argument stands up to scrutiny, once one gives attention to it.

On this showing, the syntax of *The Prelude* is not doing what it offers to do. It seems to be explaining, while in fact it is meditating, ruminating, at all events *experiencing* more fully than one does when one explains. But I am not sure that Wordsworth even pretends to explain. Elsewhere Dr. Leavis makes the point like this:

> Even if there were not so much poetry to hold the mind in a subtly incompatible mode of attention, it would still be difficult to continue attending to the philosophic argument, because of the way in which the verse, evenly meditative in tone and movement, goes on and on, without dialectical suspense and crisis or rise and fall. By an innocently insidious trick Wordsworth, in this calm ruminative progression, will appear to be preoccupied with a scrupulous nicety of statement, with a judicial weighing of alternative possibilities, while actually making it more difficult to check the argument from which he will emerge, as it were inevitably, with a far from inevitable conclusion.

Here the expression, "an innocently insidious trick," sends us back to the idea of Wordsworth's syntax as somehow conjuror's patter. On the other hand the "movement" that "goes on and on without dialectical suspense and crisis or rise and fall" is, it seems, one of the elements that work against argument. And this movement (this is my point) is as much a movement of syntax, a movement of the mind, as it is a movement in the ear. "Dialectical" admits as much. The syntax therefore presents what is really going on, meditation, not argument; and it is therefore authentic, not a play of misleading forms. This confirms me in my original explanation: that this is largely a poetry of verbal symbols which must be taken on trust (almost but not quite like notes or chords in music), for the sake of the articulations jointed between them.

II

Mr. Empson and Dr. Leavis, I suggest, were wrong to think that this poetry aimed at even the effect of philosophic argument. That Wordsworth thought, at Coleridge's instigation, that he might be a philosophic poet is here beside the point; we are speaking of what the poetry does, not of what the poet intended it to do. And in any case, this is the prelude to a philosophic poem, not the poem itself. When that poem appeared, the poetry was not of this kind, as Dr. Leavis acknowledges—"the doctrinal passages of *The Excursion* . . . are plain enough."

The critics were misled, not by the syntax of *The Prelude*, but by its vocabulary, which appears to be "abstract." It is certainly more "abstract" than a great deal of English poetry, but as I have argued, it is not abstract in any strict sense. Its ˙rbs are concrete, and its nouns are verbal symbols, neither concre   ˙or abstract. That it was the vocabulary that got in Dr. Leavis's wa˙ s proved, I think, by his admission that, for him, the Hartleian poem of 1805–6 gives more the effect of philosophic argument than the revised version of 1850. Dr. Leavis presents what he calls "a representative improvement," by printing a passage in both the versions. At the risk of being tedious, I shall present both passages, and consider Dr. Leavis's comments on them. First, the version of 1805–6 (Book Two, lines 237–266):

> Bless'd the infant Babe,
> (For with my best conjectures I would trace
> The progress of our Being) blest the Babe,
> Nurs'd in his Mother's arms, the Babe who sleeps
> Upon his Mother's breast, who, when his soul
> Claims manifest kindred with an earthly soul,
> Doth gather passion from his Mother's eye!
> Such feelings pass into his torpid life
> Like an awakening breeze, and hence his mind
> Even [in the first trial of its powers]
> Is prompt and watchful, eager to combine
> In one appearance, all the elements
> And parts of the same object, else detach'd
> And loth to coalesce. Thus day by day,
> Subjected to the discipline of love,
> His organs and recipient faculties
> Are quicken'd, are more vigorous, his mind spreads,
> Tenacious of the forms which it receives.
> In one beloved presence, nay and more
> In that most apprehensive habitude
> And those sensations which have been deriv'd
> From this beloved Presence, there exists

> A virtue which irradiates and exalts
> All objects through all intercourse of sense.
> No outcast, he, bewilder'd and depress'd:
> Along his infant veins are interfus'd
> The gravitation and the filial bond
> Of nature, that connect him with the world.
> Emphatically such a Being lives,
> An inmate of this *active* universe.

In 1850 this becomes (Book Two, lines 233–254):

> Blest the infant Babe,
> (For with my best conjecture I would trace
> Our Being's earthly progress) blest the Babe,
> Nursed in his Mother's arms, who sinks to sleep
> Rocked on his Mother's breast; who with his soul
> Drinks in the feelings of his Mother's eye!
> For him, in one dear Presence, there exists
> A virtue which irradiates and exalts
> Objects through widest intercourse of sense.
> No outcast he, bewildered and depressed:
> Along his infant veins are interfused
> The gravitation and the filial bond
> Of nature that connect him with the world.
> Is there a flower, to which he points with hand
> Too weak to gather it, already love
> Drawn from love's purest earthly fount for him
> Hath beautified that flower; already shades
> Of pity cast from inward tenderness
> Do fall around him upon aught that bears
> Unsightly marks of violence or harm.
> Emphatically such a Being lives
> Frail creature as he is, helpless as frail,
> An inmate of this active universe.

Dr. Leavis remarks, "No one is likely to dispute that the later version is decidedly the more satisfactory." However, I mean to dispute it.

I prefer the earlier version in the first place because it does more to deserve that "active" which in 1805 got italics denied to it in 1850. Not only are there more active verbs in the first version, but they are more energetic. In 1805 the child *claims* kindred and *gathers* passion, where in 1850 he "drinks in" feeling. His mind *spreads*, is eager to combine, tenacious and *apprehensive*. (The Latinate pun delivers the muscular grasp of the policeman apprehending the lag.) The later version is mawkish, emphasizing the frailty of the child, his weakness. In the first version the Mother's love is an energy, comparable with the force of gravitation and the chemical force that stirs the torpid life. ("Torpid," of course, was a technical term of eighteenth-century science.) In the later version, the Mother's love is presented as tenderness, and even then as combined or confused with pity. The "gravitation," which survives into the later version, is out of place there, in a context of imagery that is predominantly and weakly visual ("*shades* of pity"), where at first it had been muscular and dynamic. The pseudo-syntax of the rhetorical question ("Is there a flower . . . ?") goes along with this pervasive slackening of tension, this retarded and unsteadied movement.

If I ask myself what grounds Dr. Leavis can have for preferring the later version, I can only suppose he is attracted by the relative concreteness (heaven knows it is phantasmal enough) of the flower and even the "Unsightly marks of violence or harm." I would sum up the difference between these two versions by saying that, in the earlier draft, Wordsworth is rendering the experience of being a child at the mother's breast. He is doing this in the only way possible, from inside the child's mind, by rendering in his verse the movements of the child's consciousness, stirring here, checked or sluggish there, drawn this way by powerful currents, dammed back somewhere else. In the later version the poet is sometimes inside the child's mind, sometimes inside the mother's, sometimes inside the spectator's; and by thus shifting his point of view, he denies himself the chance of rendering with fidelity the movements in the child's mind or the mother's or the spectator's. Undoubtedly the language of the earlier version appears more abstract, but it is not therefore ratiocinative. It seems to me that its strength is all in its energetic verbs, and the nouns that attend them ("powers," "elements," "parts," "forms," "sensations," "objects") are correspondingly thin and general. And of course this energy in representing movements of the mind fits in with the fact that Hartley, Wordsworth's master here, was the last of the mechanic psychologists such as influenced Pope, who explained the movements of the mind in terms drawn ultimately from mechanics.

Mr. John Jones, in his very valuable book on Wordsworth, *The

Egotistical Sublime, has lately insisted on the extent to which Wordsworth always thought in these eighteenth-century terms:

> There is . . . a conservatism in the context of Wordsworth's thought. He is not in revolt against the Great Machine, the master-image of eighteenth-century science and philosophy. Only the phrase is unwordsworthian (though there is enough of pure eighteenth-century poetic in him to allow a reference to his wife's spirit, in relation to her body, as "the very pulse of the machine"): he would prefer something more supple, like "this universal frame of things." His complaint is that nobody has as yet observed its component parts with sufficiently devoted care, or experienced fully the power and beauty of its movement.
>
> In *The Prelude*, Wordsworth uses the word "things" with astonishing frequency. The Concordance reveals that the 1850 text alone accounts for about one-third of its occcurrences in the entire bulk of his poetry. "I looked for universal things"; "I conversed with things that really are"; Wordsworth will make his verse "deal boldly with substantial things"—the word is clearly and consistently referred to the main theme of the poem. His search for universal things is on one side a search for particularity: in his insistence upon constancy, boundedness, irreducibility, he betrays the imaginative impression of a traditional English materialism. But he is more than a materialist, in that he enquires not only for the particular but for the powerful. Here his resources are heavily taxed. In order to express essential energy, he is too often led to personify spirit, motion, power itself, in a context of vague declamation.

But Wordsworth can do better than that. In passages such as the one just considered, of 1805, he conveys the power as well as the particularity, the different kinds of pulse in the natural machine, by the precisely discriminated energies of his verbs, which concretely act out the powers he is speaking of. In him perhaps one may applaud what Fenollosa applauded in Shakespeare, his "persistent, natural, and magnificent use of hundreds of transitive verbs."

The Romance of Nature and the Negative Way

Geoffrey Hartman

We know from "Tintern Abbey" that in certain "blessed" moods, the eye is quieted. Book Twelve of *The Prelude* [references are to the 1850 version, unless otherwise noted] relates that the tyranny of sight was, as well as "almost inherent in the creature," especially oppressive at a particular point in Wordsworth's life. This time coincided with an excessive sitting in judgment and may safely be identified with the period when the poet, disillusioned by the French Revolution and with Godwin, sought formal proof in everything till "yielding up moral questions in despair":

> I speak in recollection of a time
> When the bodily eye, in every stage of life
> The most despotic of our senses, gained
> Such strength in *me* as often held my mind
> In absolute dominion.
>
> (XII. 127 ff.)

He refuses to enter upon abstruse argument to show how Nature thwarted such despotism by summoning all the senses to counteract each other; but his reflections lead him somewhat later in the same book to think of those "spots of time" which preserved and renovated him. One of them is the famous episode of the young boy, separated

From *The Unmediated Vision*, © 1954 by Yale University and © 1982 by Geoffrey Hartman, and from *Wordsworth's Poetry 1787–1814*, © 1964 by Yale University. Yale University Press, 1964.

from his companion on a ride in the hills, dismounting out of fear and stumbling onto a murderer's gibbet, mouldered down, and of which nothing remained except the murderer's name carved nearby and kept clean because of local superstition:

> The grass is cleared away, and to this hour
> The characters are fresh and visible:
> A casual glance had shown them, and I fled,
> Faltering and faint, and ignorant of the road:
> Then, reascending the bare common, saw
> A naked pool that lay beneath the hills,
> The beacon on the summit, and, more near,
> A girl, who bore a pitcher on her head,
> And seemed with difficult steps to force her way
> Against the blowing wind. It was, in truth,
> An ordinary sight.
>
> (XII. 244 ff.)

The nudity of such scenes has often been remarked and various hypotheses invented, for example that Wordsworth lacked sexual sensibility, saw in Nature a father substitute, etc. But a correct detailing of the characteristics of this moment would have to note first the cause of the faltering and fleeing, which is not so much the mouldered gibbet as the fresh and visible characters engraved by an unknown hand. The name evidently doesn't matter, only the characters as characters, and the effect on the boy is swift and out of proportion to the simple sight, a casual glance sufficing. Suggested first is the indestructibility of human consciousness, exemplified by the new characters, and after that the indestructibility of a consciousness in Nature, figured in the skeletal characters of a scene denuded of all color, sketched in a permanent black and white, yet capable of immense physical impact. The mystical chord is touched, and the eye overpowered by an intuition of characters affecting no single sense but compelling a comparison between the indestructibility of human consciousness and a physical indestructibilty. The same effect will be found suggested in the second of the spots of time:

> I sate half-sheltered by a naked wall;
> Upon my right hand couched a single sheep,
> Upon my left a blasted hawthorn stood;
>
> (XII. 299 ff.)

and the description of the characters of the great Apocalpyse likewise starts with an intuition of indestructibility:

the immeasurable height
Of woods decaying, never to be decayed
(VI. 624 ff.)

This, moreover, is coupled with a hint of the Last Judgment in the trumpeting of waterfalls that to the eye seem to possess the rigidity of rock,

The stationary blasts of waterfalls.

But before reaching a conclusion we should consider one more event, the most significant perhaps that enters through, yet overpowers, the eye. Wandering among London crowds the poet is smitten

Abruptly, with the view (a sight not rare)
Of a blind Beggar, who, with upright face,
Stood, propped against a wall, upon his chest
Wearing a written paper, to explain
His story, whence he came, and who he was.
Caught by the spectacle my mind turned round
As with the might of waters; and apt type
This label seemed of the utmost we can know,
Both of ourselves and of the universe;
And, on the shape of that unmoving man,
His steadfast face and sightless eyes, I gazed,
As if admonished from another world.
(VII. 638 ff.)

As in the gibbet scene, the poet emphasizes that the sight was ordinary and sudden, that is, having no intrinsic claim on the mind, nor worked up by meditation. But a greater similarity obtains between the two, though it is by no means complete. Both events focus on a label written by an impersonal hand. But whereas the characters in the one case seem indestructible, here the label is a sign of human impotence. Yet the superficial label clearly points to a set of deeper and indestructible characters, for the suggestion is that the lost eyes of the beggar were only like a piece of paper, a visual surface, and that, being removed, they leave the man more steadfast, fixed, eternal. We rediscover Wordsworth's constant concern with denudation, stemming from both a fear of visual reality and a desire for physical indestructibility. And the fine image of the mind turned by the spectacle as if with the might of waters, refers to that vast identity established throughout the poems of Wordsworth, an identity against sight, its fever and triviality, and making all things tend to the sound of universal waters; subduing the eyes by a power of harmony, and the reason by the suggestion of a Final Judgment which is God's alone. The intuition of indestructibility in the midst of decay, and the identity of the power in light with the power of sound ("by form or image unprofaned") are the two modes of a vision in which the mind knows itself almost without exterior cause or else as no less real, here, no less indestructible than the object of its perceptions.

II

Nature, for Wordsworth, is not an "object" but a presence and a power; a motion and a spirit; not something to be worshiped and consumed, but always a guide leading beyond itself. This guidance starts in earliest childhood. The boy of *Prelude* I is fostered alike by beauty and by fear. Through beauty, nature often makes the boy feel at home, for, as in the Great Ode, his soul is alien to this world. But through fear, nature reminds the boy from where he came, and prepares him, having lost heaven, also to lose nature. The boy of *Prelude* I, who does not yet know he must suffer this loss as well, is warned by nature itself of the solitude to come.

I have suggested elsewhere how the fine skating scene of the first book (425–63), though painted for its own sake, to capture the animal spirits of children spurred by a clear and frosty night, moves from vivid images of immediate life to an absolute calm which foreshadows a deeper and more hidden life. The Negative Way is a gradual one, and the child is weaned by a premonitory game of hide-and-seek in which nature changes its shape from familiar to unfamiliar, or even fails the child. There is a great fear, either in Wordsworth or in nature, of traumatic breaks: *Natura non facit saltus*.

If the child is led by nature to a more deeply mediated understanding of nature, the mature singer who composes *The Prelude* begins with that understanding or even beyond it—with the spontaneously creative spirit. Wordsworth plunges into *medias res*, where the *res* is Poetry, or Nature only insofar as it has guided him to a height whence he must find his own way. But Book Six, with which we are immediately concerned, records what is chronologically an intermediate period, in which the first term is neither Nature nor Poetry. It is Imagination in embryo: the mind muted yet also strengthened by the external world's opacities. Though imagination is with Wordsworth on the journey of 1790, nature seems particularly elusive. He goes out to a nature which seems to hide as in the crossing of the Alps.

The first part of this episode is told to illustrate a curious melancholy related to the "presence" of imagination and the "absence" of nature. Like the young Apollo in Keats's *Hyperion*, Wordsworth is strangely dissatisfied with the riches before him, and compelled to seek some other region:

> Where is power?
> Whose hand, whose essence, what divinity
> Makes this alarum in the elements,
> While I here idle listen on the shores
> In fearless yet in aching ignorance?

To this soft or "luxurious" sadness, a more masculine kind is added, which results from a "stern mood" or "underthirst of vigor"; and it is in order to throw light on this further melancholy that Wordsworth tells the incident of his crossing the Alps.

The stern mood to which Wordsworth refers can only be his premonition of spiritual autonomy, of an independence from sense-experience foreshadowed by nature since earliest childhood. It is the 'underground' form of imagination, and *Prelude* II.315 ff. describes it as "an obscure sense/Of possible sublimity," for which the soul, remembering *how* it felt in exalted moments, but no longer *what* it felt, continually strives to find a new content. The element of obscurity, related to nature's self-concealment, is necessary to the soul's capacity for growth, for it vexes the latter toward self-dependence. Childhood pastures become viewless; the soul cannot easily find the source from which it used to drink the visionary power; and while dim memories of a passionate commerce with external things drive it more than ever to the world, this world makes itself more than ever inscrutable. The travelers' separation from their guides, then that of the road from the stream (VI.568), and finally their trouble with the peasant's words that have to be "translated," express subtly the soul's desire for a *beyond*. Yet only when poet, brook, and road are once again "fellow-travellers" (VI.622), and Wordsworth holds to Nature, does that reveal—a Proteus in the grasp of the hero—its prophecy.

This prophecy was originally the second part of the adventure, the delayed vision which compensates for his disappointment (the "Characters of the great Apocalypse," VI.617–40). In its original sequence, therefore, the episode has only two parts: the first term or moment of natural immediacy is omitted, and we go straight to the second term, the inscrutability of an external image, which leads via the gloomy strait to its renewal. Yet, as if this pattern demanded a substitute third term, Wordsworth's tribute to "Imagination" severs the original temporal sequence, and forestalls nature's renewal of the bodily eye with ecstatic praise of the inner eye.

The apocalypse of the gloomy strait loses by this the character of a *terminal* experience. Nature is again surpassed, for the poet's imagination is called forth, at the time of writing, by the barely scrutable, not by the splendid emotion; by the disappointment, not the fulfillment. This (momentary) displacement of emphasis is the more effective in that the style of VI.617 ff., and the very characters of the apocalypse, suggest that the hiding places of power cannot be localized in nature. Though the apostrophe to Imagination—the special insight that comes to Wordsworth in 1804—is a real peripety, reversing a meaning already established, it is not unprepared. But it takes the poet many years to realize that nature's "end" is to lead to something "without end," to teach the travelers to transcend nature.

The three parts of this episode, therefore, can help us understand the mind's growth toward independence of immediate external stimuli. The measure of that independence is Imagination, and carries with it a precarious self-consciousness. We see that the mind must pass through a stage where it experiences Imagination as a power separate from Nature, that the poet must come to think and feel as if by his own choice, or from the structure of his mind.

VI-a (557–91) shows the young poet still dependent on the immediacy of the external world. Imagination frustrates that dependence secretly, yet its blindness toward nature is accompanied by a blindness toward itself. It is only a "mute Influence of the soul, / An Element of nature's inner self" (1805, VIII. 513–14).

VI-b (592–616) gives an example of thought or feeling that came from the poet's mind without immediate external excitement. There remains, of course, the memory of VI-a (the disappointment), but this is an internal feeling, not an external image. The poet recognizes at last that the power he has looked for in the outside world is really within and frustrating his search. A shock of recognition then feeds the very blindness toward the external world which helped to produce that shock.

In VI-c (617–40) the landscape is again an immediate external object of experience. The mind cannot separate in it what it desires to know and what it actually knows. It is a moment of revelation, in which the poet sees not as in a glass, darkly, but face to face. VI-c clarifies, therefore, certain details of VI-a and *seems* to actualize figurative details of VI-b. The matter-of-fact interplay of quick and lingering movement, of up-and-down perplexities in the ascent (VI.567 ff.), reappears in larger letters; while the interchanges of light and darkness, of cloud and cloudlessness, of rising like a vapor from the abyss and pouring like a flood from heaven have entered the landscape bodily. The gloomy strait also participates in this actualization. It is revealed as the secret middle term which leads from the barely scrutable presence of nature to its resurrected image. The travelers who move freely with or against the terrain, hurrying upward, pacing downward, perplexed at crossings, are now led narrowly by the pass as if it were their rediscovered guide.

The Prelude, as history of a poet's mind, foresees the time when the "Characters of the great Apocalypse" will be intuited without the medium of nature. The time approaches even as the poet writes, and occasionally cuts across his narrative, the imagination rising up, as in Book Six, "Before the eye and progress of my Song" (version of 1805). This phrase, at once conventional and exact, suggests that imagination waylaid the poet on his mental journey. The "eye" of his song, trained on a temporal sequence with the vision in the strait as its final term, is suddenly obscured. He is momentarily forced to deny nature that magnificence it had shown in the gloomy strait, and to attribute the glory to imagination, whose interposition in the very moment of writing proves it to be a power more independent than nature of time and place, and so a better type "Of first, and last, and midst, and without end" (VI.640).

We know that VI-b records something that happened during composition, and which enters the poem as a new biographical event. Wordsworth has just described his disappointment (VI-a) and turns in anticipation to nature's compensatory finale (VI-c). He is about to respect the original temporal sequence, "the eye and progress" of his song. But as he looks forward, in the moment of composition, from blankness toward revelation, a new insight cuts him off from the latter. The original disappointment is seen not as a test, or as a prelude to magnificence, but as a revelation in itself. It suddenly reveals a power—imagination—that could not be satisfied by anything in nature, however sublime. The song's progress comes to a halt because the poet is led beyond nature. Unless he can respect the natural (which includes the temporal) order, his song, at least as narrative, must cease. Here Imagination, not Nature (as in I.96 ff.), defeats Poetry.

This conclusion may be verified by comparing the versions of 1805 and 1850. The latter replaces "Before the eye and progress of my Song" with a more direct metaphorical transposition. Imagination is said to rise from the mind's abyss "Like an unfathered vapour that enwraps, / At once, some lonely traveller." The (literal) traveler of 1790 becomes the (mental) traveler at the moment of composition. And though one Shakespearean doublet has disappeared, another implicitly takes its place: does not imagination rise from "the dark backward and abysm of time" (*The Tempest*, I.2.50)? The result, in any case, is a disorientation of time added to that of way; an apocalyptic moment in which past and future overtake the present; and the poet, cut off from nature by imagination, is, in an absolute sense, lonely.

The last stage in the poet's "progress" has been reached. The travelers of VI-a had already left behind their native land, the public rejoicing of France, rivers, hills, and spires; they have separated from their guides, and finally from the unbridged mountain stream. Now, in 1804, imagination separates the poet from all else: human companionship, the immediate scene, the remembered scene. The end of the *via negativa* is near. There is no more "eye and progress"; the invisible progress of VI-a (Wordsworth crossing the Alps unknowingly) has revealed itself as a progress independent of visible ends, or engendered by the desire for an "invisible world"—the substance of things hoped for, the evidence of things not seen. Wordsworth descants on the Pauline definition of faith:

> in such strength
> Of usurpation, when the light of sense
> Goes out, but with a flash that has revealed
> The invisible world, doth greatness make abode,
> There harbours; whether we be young or old,

> Our destiny, our being's heart and home,
> Is with infinitude, and only there;
> With hope it is, hope that can never die,
> Effort, and expectation, and desire,
> And something evermore about to be.
> (VI.599–608)

Any further possibility of progress for the poet would be that of song itself, of poetry no longer subordinate to the mimetic function, the experience faithfully traced to this height. The poet is a traveler insofar as he must respect nature's past guidance and retrace his route. He did come, after all, to an important instance of bodily vision. The way is the song. But the song often strives to become the way. And when this happens, when the song seems to capture the initiative, in such supreme moments of poetry as VI-b or even VI-c, the way is lost. Nature in VI-c shows "Winds thwarting winds, bewildered and forlorn," as if they too had lost their way. The apocalypse in the gloomy strait depicts a self-thwarting march and counter-march of elements, a divine mockery of the concept of the Single Way.

But in VI-c, nature still stands over and against the poet; he is still the observer, the eighteenth-century gentleman admiring a new manifestation of the sublime, even if the lo! or mark! is supressed. He moves haltingly but he moves; and the style of the passage emphasizes continuities. Yet with the imagination athwart there is no movement, no looking before and after. The song itself must be the way, though that of a blinded man, who admits, "I was lost." Imagination, as it shrouds the poet's eye, also shrouds the eye of his song, whose tenor is nature guiding and fostering the power of song.

It is not, therefore, till 1804 that Wordsworth discovers the identity of his hidden guide. VI-c was probably composed in 1799, and it implies that Wordsworth, at that time, still thought nature his guide. But now he sees that it was imagination moving him by means of nature, just as Beatrice guided Dante by means of Virgil. It is not nature as such but nature indistinguishably blended with imagination that compels the poet along his Negative Way. Yet, if VI-b prophesies against the world of sense-experience, Wordsworth's affection and point of view remain unchanged. Though his discovery shakes the foundation of his poem, he returns after a cloudburst of verses to the pedestrian attitude of 1790, when the external world

and not imagination seemed to be his guide ("Our journey we re-
newed, / Led by the stream," etc.). Moreover, with the exception
of VI-b, imagination does not move the poet directly, but always
through the agency of nature. The childhood "Visitings of imaginative power" depicted in Books One and Twelve also appeared in
the guise or disguise of nature. Wordsworth's journey as a poet can
only continue with eyes, but the imagination experienced as a power
distinct from nature opens his eyes by putting them out. Wordsworth, therefore, does not adhere to nature because of natural fact,
but despite it and because of human and poetic fact. Imagination is
indeed an *awe-full* power.

III

Wordsworth's attempt to revive the Romance mode for a consciously Protestant imagination had no issue in his own poetry, or
even in English poetry as a whole, which will follow the freer rom-
ances of Keats, Shelley, and Scott. But in America, where Puritanism
still questioned the sacred and also secular rights of imagination, a
similar development is found. The possibility of a consciously Protestant romance is what inspires or self-justifies Hawthorne, Melville,
and Henry James. If the Christian poets of the Renaissance wondered
how they could use Pagan forms and themes, the neo-Puritan writers
wonder how they can use the Christian superstitions. Not only do
we find the often directly presented schism between an old-world
and a new-world imagination, in which the old world is, sometimes
nobly, under the spell of "superstitious fancies strong," but the action
centers on the manner in which a strange central apparition, a romance phenomenon, is imaginatively valued. In the European society
in which she moves, James's Daisy Miller is a white doe, and there
are those who do the gentle creature wrong, who kill her, in fact,
by knowing her wrongly. I have chosen, of course, a very simple
case; but there is no need to ascend the scale of Jamesian or Melvillean
fiction to the final white mystery. Wordsworth's scruples concerning
the imagination are Puritan scruples even though they are gradually
associated with Anglican thought.

That Wordsworth was seeking to develop a new kind of romance, one that would chasten our imaginations, is already suggested
by the stanzas dedicating *The White Doe* to his wife. A moving
personal document, they trace the history of his relation to romantic
fiction. He describes his and Mary's love of Spencer, their innocent

enjoyment of "each specious miracle." But then a "lamentable change"—the death of Wordsworth's brother—pierces their hearts:

> For us the stream of fiction ceased to flow,
> For us the voice of melody was mute.

Romance and realism are suddenly opposed. The truth is too harsh, and fiction is even blamed for deceiving the mind, for veiling reality with "the light that never was." Spenser, however, is so soothing, that he beguiles them once more, and the story of the Nortons, with its own "mild Una in her sober cheer," is composed.

But the death of Wordsworth's brother leaves its mark. Though Wordsworth returns to Spencer, the stream of fiction is troubled, it will never again flow lightly "in the bent of Nature." The poet seems to have interpreted his brother's death, like his father's, as a "chastisement" following an over-extension of imaginative hopes (cf. *Prelude* XII. 309–16). The dream of happiness built on John's return was something *hyper moron*, secretly apocalyptic, or beyond the measure nature could fulfill. This is not to say that John's loss was the decisive cause for Wordsworth's decline as a poet—I have abjured speculation on this matter. Some speculations, however, are simply a way of describing the later poetry, and it is quite true that whether or not the decisive shock came in 1805, Wordsworth's mind is now much less inclined to "wanton" in "the exercise of its own powers . . . loving its own creation." If we compare his dedicatory stanzas to Mary with those Shelley wrote to *his* Mary and which preface "The Witch of Atlas," the distance between one poet's lighthearted espousal of "visonary rhyme" and the other's weight of scruples becomes fully apparent. It is as if Shelley and Wordsworth had polarized Spenserian romance, the former taking its *dulce*, the latter, its *utile*.

It might not seem possible that the later poetry could be beset by even more scruples, but this is what happens. Wordsworth's attitude toward his mind's "exercise of its powers" suffers a further restraint. He begins to watch on *two* fronts: to be deluded that "the mighty Deep / Was even the gentlest of all gentle things" is as dangerous as to gaze into the bottomless abyss. He is now as careful about an idealizing impulse as about the apocalyptic intimation. The presence of a Sympathetic Nature, which is the one superstition for which he had kept his respect, for it is vital not only to poetry but also to human development, being a necessary illusion in the growth of the mind, this too is falling away. Yet the story of the white doe is his attempt to save the notion once more in some purer form. He knows that to give it up entirely is to return to a holy, but stern and melancholy, imagination.

Under the pressure of these many restraints, Wordsworth's mind has little chance to fall in love with or explore its own impressions. Self-discovery, which informs the meditative lyrics (the act of recall there is never a passive thing but verges on new and often disturbing intuitions) almost disappears. And, by a curious irony, the unpublished *Prelude*, which is his greatest testimony to the living mind, now discourages further self-exploration. Such later sentiments as:

> Earth prompts—Heaven urges; let us seek the light,
> Studious of that pure intercourse begun
> When first our infant brows their lustre won,

do not rely, in their weakness, on the external authority of the church, but on the internal authority of his own greatest poem, which is kept private, and as scripture to himself abets the flat reiteration of his ideas in a slew of minor poems. J. M. Murry is right in feeling that the later Wordsworth represents the process of self-discovery as much more orthodox from the beginning than it was; and Coleridge, severely disappointed by *The Excursion*, offers a similar diagnosis: Wordsworth's opinions, he said, were based on "self-established convictions" and did not have for readers in general the special force they had for the poet.

There are, nevertheless, strange happenings in the later poetry, which has a precarious quality of its own. Though Wordsworth no longer dallies with surmise, he cannot entirely forego apocalyptic fancies, or the opposite (if more generous) error which attributes to nature a vital and continuous role in the maturing of the mind. The old imaginative freedoms continue to rise up, like Proteus or Triton, against the narrow-minded materialism of his time—a living Pagan is better than a dead Christian spirit. He is not beyond being surprised by his imagination. It continues to defy his censorship, even if he queries every fancy, every moment of "quickened subjectivity." I shall conclude by considering certain incidents from the later poetry that show in what relation to his own mind Wordsworth stands.

In 1820, thirty years after his journey through the Alps, he takes Mary and Dorothy to the Continent. Dorothy keeps her usual journal, to which he probably turned in composing the "memorials" of that tour. While in the valley of Chamonix (a place sacred to the poet) the travelers hear voices rising from the mountain's base and glimpse below them a procession making its way to the church. Dorothy describes the scene for us:

> [we saw] a lengthening Procession—the Priest in his robes— the host, and banners uplifted; and men following two and two;—and, last of all, a great number of females, in like order; the head and body of each covered with a white garment. The stream continued to flow on for a long time, till all had paced slowly round the church. . . . The procession was grave and simple, agreeing with the simple decorations of a village church; the banners made no glittering shew; the Females composed a moving girdle round the Church; their figures, from head to foot, covered with one piece of white cloth, resembled the small pyramids of the Glacier, which were before our eyes; and it was impossible to look at one and the other without fancifully connecting them together. Imagine the *moving* Figures, like a stream of pyramids,—the white Church, the half-concealed Village, and the Glacier close behind, among pine-trees,—a pure sun shining over all! and remember that these objects were seen at the base of those enormous mountains, and you may have some faint notion of the effect produced upon us by that beautiful spectacle.

Wordsworth is inspired by this to a 'progress poem' entitled "Processions. Suggested on a Sabbath Morning in the Vale of Chamouny" which traces the spirit of religious ceremonies from ancient times to the present. The Alps, archaic strongholds, allow him to recognize in Pagan ritual the impure basis of Christian pageantry. Shrill canticles have yielded to sober litanies; silver bells and pompous decorations to "hooded vestments fair"; and noisy feasts to an assembly breathing "a Spirit more subdued and soft." Moreover, as he looks on, another archaic vestige suggests itself, which is hinted at in Dorothy's account: that the procession is born of the mountain, like the white pillars above it. Indeed, the glacier columns, juxtaposed with the moving column of white figures, bring to mind the theory of Creation by Metamorphosis. The mountain, in this Blakean insight, is "men seen afar."

Wordsworth is strangely frightened at this—not at the mere

thought of metamorphosis but at a reflexive knowledge connected with it. He realizes he has viewed more than a transformed archaic ritual, or ancient truth: he has seen the *source* of that truth in his mind's excited and spontaneous joining of the living stream of people to the frozen of nature. As in his greatest poetry, the mind is moved by itself after being moved by something external. He writes a stanza similar in tenor and directness to the apostrophe to Imagination in the sixth book of *The Prelude*, similar at least in its magnificent opening:

> Trembling, I look upon the secret springs
> Of that licentious craving in the mind
> To act the God among external things,
> To bind, on apt suggestion, or unbind;
> And marvel not that antique Faith inclined
> To crowd the world with metamorphosis,
> Vouchsafed in pity or in wrath assigned;
> Such insolent temptations wouldst thou miss,
> Avoid these sights; nor brood o'er Fable's dark abyss!

Wordsworth's reaction, visceral first, pontific later, differs from the usual religious decision to relinquish a profane subject or style. He does not say, in Herbert's sweet manner, farewell dark fables, or censor their use in Christian poetry. But he turns in the moment, and explicitly, from a power of his own mind without which poetry is not conceivable. It is not fabling merely, but "Fable's dark abyss"— the mind of man itself—he now fears to look on. He is afraid of fables because of their reaction on a mind that might brood too pregnantly on what they reveal of its power. Yet at the time of *The White Doe* he had still tried to 'convert' a fable by purifying its superstition and cleansing its mystery: the doe is not a metamorphosed spirit and her powers of sympathy are due to natural not supernatural causes. What a difference, also, between this sacred tremor and his earlier, almost cavalier attitude toward all mythologies! In 1798, and again in 1814, he professes to be unalarmed at their conceptions because of the greater "fear and awe" that fall on him when he regards "the Mind of Man— / My haunt, and the main region of my song." He did not fear his fear then as he does now, trembling before his own creative will.

Wordsworth's diffidence is no sudden thing; we found it at the beginning of his career, and related it to an extraordinary, apocalyptic consciousness of self. At that time religion seemed to him too much a product of that same apocalyptic consciousness. Nature had to be defended against a supernatural religion as well as against the barren eye of Science. Was it ever meant, he asks,

> That this majestic imagery, the clouds
> The ocean and the firmament of heaven
> Should lie a barren picture on the mind?

In the later poetry, however, religion has changed its role. It now protects rather than threatens nature. He begins to identify with the Anglo-Catholic concept of the *via media* his ideal of Nature, of England, even of Poetry. The poet, he had said in 1802, is "the rock of defence for human nature; an upholder and preserver, carrying everywhere with him relationship and love." He now sees the church as part of that rock: an *ecclesia* mediating by a divine principle of mercy the sterner demands of God, State, and Imagination, demands which have often threatened human nature, and led to individual or collective fanaticisms. Religion and imagination are intervolved (Wordsworth and Blake are in perfect accord on *this*), and whereas Catholicism incites an apocalyptic response:

> Mine ear has rung, my spirit sunk subdued,
> Sharing the strong emotion of the crowd,
> When each pale brow to dread hosannas bowed
> While clouds of incense mounting veiled the rood,
> That glimmered like a pine-tree dimly viewed
> Through Alpine vapours

the Anglican Church, which is the *religio loci* corresponding to the *genius loci* of England, rejects such appalling rites in the hope that nature, man, and God constitute ultimately "one society":

> the Sun with his first smile
> Shall greet that symbol crowning the low Pile:
> And the fresh air of incense-breathing morn
> Shall wooingly embrace it; and green moss
> Creep round its arms through centuries unborn.

Covenant has replaced, as completely as possible, apocalypse: his emblem marries nature, time, and the spirit.

The *Ecclesiastical Sonnets*, from which the above extracts are taken, show Wordsworth is suspicious of everything that could rouse the apocalyptic passions. This is also an important clue to his later politics, which seem illiberal, apostate even; a failure of nerve like his poetry. The evidence against him is indeed black. "That such a man," cries Shelley, "should be such a poet!" Shelley did not know Wordsworth personally, but even the faithful Crabb Robinson, who made all the possible allowances, is compelled to address Dorothy in 1827: "I assure you it gives me a real pain when I think that some further commentator may possibly hereafter write: 'This great poet survived to the fifth decennary of the nineteenth century but he appears to have died in the year 1814, as far as life consisted in an active sympathy with the temporary [viz. temporal] welfare of his fellow-creatures.' " Only in matters of Church doctrine, as distinguished from Church or national politics, does something of Wordsworth's liberalism remain. His views, says H. N. Fairchild, praising where he thinks to blame, are "wholly consistent with modern Christian liberalism . . . very loose and vague, however, for a nineteenth-century High Churchman."

Wordsworth, it is clear, has passed from the idea that change (let alone revolutionary change) intends a repossession of the earth to the idea that it might cause a greater dispossession than ever. Harper has documented his panic fear of change. It is a deeply emotional and imaginative thing, and has almost no relation to his own very small prosperity. The Reform Bill of 1832, for instance, seems to him to herald a revolt of the masses. He prophesies ruin and destruction to England and thinks of having to leave it. His jeremiads indicate a soul which knows itself too well, and is still afraid in others of those "blasts of music" and "daring sympathies with power" to which he had given ear at the time of the French Revolution.

Dark thoughts—"blind thoughts" as he calls them in "Resolution and Independence"—certainly continue to impinge on him. Yet how deep they lie, almost too deep for notice. They come to the surface only in matters of politics, and in exceptionally self-conscious verses, like those in memory of Chamonix. The most famous of the River Duddon sonnets, the "After-thought" of the series, runs truer to course. The whole series, less conventional than it seems, participates in the poet's desire to bind together the powers of his mind and of nature; and to know this illumines the character of his final sonnet.

The "After-thought" begins very simply:

> I thought of Thee, my partner and my guide,
> As being passed away.

It makes us wonder, this quiet human directness, whom the poet is addressing, but then Willard Sperry's observation that "his brief for nature's morality was based upon her openness to our address" comes to mind. The more remarkable aspect of the verses is what Wordsworth can have meant by the river "passing away."

He must have recalled the prophecy of streams shrinking in the final fire, of "Old Ocean, in his bed left singed and bare." This must have come to him and threatened the entire basis of his sonnets, which is the partnership of mind and nature. Or is it his own death which he foresaw, as in "Tintern Abbey"? But why, in that case, would he talk of Duddon's death rather than of his own?

I suspect, in any case, that the personal fact of his dying seemed to him a small matter compared to the river's loss and the foreboded severing of the loves of man and nature. Duddon is mortal in that it may die in man or to him as he grows older, but especially in that it may die to the human imagination, generally, on Wordsworth's death. For if his special mission among poets is to marry nature to the mind, his death takes on a cosmic meaning. The rest of the poem, of course, dispels his strange fear concerning Duddon:

> —Vain sympathies!
> For, backward, Duddon! as I cast my eyes,
> I see what was, and is, and will abide;
> Still glides the Stream, and shall for ever glide;
> The Form remains, the Function never dies;
> While we, the brave, the mighty, and the wise,
> We Men, who in our morn of youth defied
> The elements, must vanish;—be it so!
> Enough, if something from our hands have power
> To live, and act, and serve the future hour;
> And if, as toward the silent tomb we go,
> Through love, through hope, and faith's transcendent dower,
> We feel that we are greater than we know.

This is pure consolation and too easy. His sympathies (for the stream!) are "vain" because nature outlives man and will continue to inspire him; and because man, too, has the promise, through religion, of an immortality that hopefully does not exclude the tie of nature.

Yet the distance between "Tintern Abbey" and the River Duddon "After-thought" is not great. The primary experience is one of nature, of the Wye or the Duddon or other great presences. In the earlier poems we are told directly of how the cataracts haunted the boy or how the objects of nature "lay upon his mind like substances" and "perplexed the bodily sense." The same kind of perplexity is produced by the appearance of the white doe. The mystery in nature is that of our relation to it, which is darkly sympathetic, so that Goethe calls it "das offenbare Geheimniss," an incumbent natural mystery. But this experience of relationship, open to all, is followed by the further mystery of its diminution, also shared by all. The poet who returns to Tintern Abbey knows his loss; he sees it in the glass of the landscape, darkly; and a prophetic fear, despite nature's continuing importance, leads him to envisage severance and even death. The conclusion that his death may mean the passing away of nature from the human mind is not yet drawn, for he prays that his sister may continue a relationship to which he is dying. But in the "after-thought" his fear touches the furthest point. It does so fleetingly, yet still bespeaks either a delusion of grandeur or a remarkable conviction that man and nature are growing irremediably apart, and that the gap between them, whether a historical error or a providential test, already verges on apocalypse. "The sun strengthens us no more, neither does the moon."

The burden of this secret consciousness in Wordsworth should not be underestimated. It is he who stands between us and the death of nature; and this is also the truest justification for the "egotistical sublime" in his poetry. He values his own lightest feeling for the sufficiencies of mother earth—

> The night that calms, the day that cheers;
> The common growth of mother-earth
> Suffices me—her tears, her mirth
> Her humblest mirth and tears

—because her call to him, unregarded, augurs a loss in our capacity to respond to nature, and hence the virtual opposite of that "great consummation" of which he sings in the verses that preface the 1814 *Excursion*. He feels that he must personally fasten or newcreate the links between nature and the human mind. The "Adonais" Shelley laments is strangely like his own conception of himself.

I may seem to exaggerate Wordsworth's sense of mission; but no one has yet explained the heart-sickness and melancholia of the aging poet. These are prompted, of course, by political fears (which are really imaginative fears) and by personal grief, yet do they differ, except in persistence, from earlier dejections? Is his "fixed despond-ency, uncorrected" human weakness merely, and the effect of old age, or may it not accord with his own younger picture of himself as a "meditative, oft a suffering man"? What his meditations were, and why linked intimately to a certain kind of suffering, may now be clear. The selfhood Wordsworth knew, and which is always re-lated to a fear of the death of nature, is at first alleviated by his sense of special mission, then cruelly confirmed by what he takes to be his growing isolation. At the time of "Michael," he is still thinking "Of youthful Poets, who among these hills / Will be my second self when I am gone"; it is in hope of these that he spins his homely ballads. But he never recognizes Shelley or Keats or any of the following generation as his second self. He is a stubborn, old, opinionated man—perhaps; the fact remains that Shelley and Keats, though con-cerned with the humanizing of imagination, have greater affinities with the Renaissance poets and that these have greater affinities with one another than Wordsworth has with any of them. Milton, whose sense of mission is as strong as his, could turn to Spencer and even to Virgil; Blake, though almost unknown in his time, thought of himself as continuing or correcting Milton and the Bible; but Words-worth, despite his love for the older writers, and especially for Mil-ton, can turn to no one in his desire to save nature for the human imagination. He is the most isolated figure among the great English poets.

The Structural Unit: "Spots of Time"

Herbert Lindenberger

> *There's not a man*
> *That lives who hath not had his godlike hours*
> *The Prelude*, III, 191–2, 1805

It is characteristic of Wordsworth's retrospective method that the reader always remains aware of two points of time, the bleak, quiet present, in which the poet sits writing to Coleridge and meditating upon the epic task imposed by his ambition to create a poem on "Nature, Man, and Society," and the deep well of the personal past to which he returns again and again so that he

> might fetch
> Invigorating thoughts from former years,
> Might fix the wavering balance of my mind,
> And haply meet reproaches, too, whose power
> May spur me on, in manhood now mature,
> To honorable toil.
>
> (I, 648–53)

This past, the quest for which in fact is the substance of *The Prelude* [references are to the 1805 version unless otherwise noted], is not re-created in and for itself, but only within the perspective of the present,

---

From *On Wordsworth's* Prelude. © 1963 by Princeton University Press.

through which alone it derives meaning. Wordsworth's method, one might say, is the antithesis of that of the historical novelist, who seeks to immerse his readers so fully in the re-created past that, if he succeeds, they lose sight of any reality outside this past. Wordsworth's past, no matter how vivid and "invigorating" it may be, never aims toward an autonomy of this sort; moreover, through the influence that the past exerts upon the present, and through his much-repeated desire to find nourishment in the past, he constantly engages in a two-way movement, back and forth, between present and past.

The characteristic form which Wordsworth developed to probe into the past is the "spot of time," a term he coined to describe two childhood incidents narrated in Book Eleven. The "spot of time" is defined in terms of its salutary effects upon him:

> There are in our existence spots of time,
> Which with distinct pre-eminence retain
> A vivifying Virtue, whence . . .
>   our minds
> Are nourished and invisibly repair'd.
>   (XI, 258–265)

But the "spot of time" can also be viewed as a literary form—one peculiar to *The Prelude* as it is not, for instance, to *The Excursion* or, for that matter, to the contemplative poetry of the preceding century. At its simplest level the "spot" is the record of a concrete past event used to illustrate some more general statements about the past. Take, for example, the passage in which Wordsworth recaptures his moment of self-dedication to poetry:

> The memory of one particular hour
> Doth here rise up against me. In a throng,
> A festal company of Maids and Youths,
> Old Men, and Matrons staid, promiscuous rout,
> A medley of all tempers, I had pass'd
> The night in dancing, gaiety and mirth;
> With din of instruments, and shuffling feet,
> And glancing forms, and tapers glittering,
> And unaim'd prattle flying up and down,
> Spirits upon the stretch, and here and there
> Slight shocks of young love-liking interspers'd,
> That mounted up like joy into the head,
> And tingled through the veins. Ere we retired,

The cock had crow'd, the sky was bright with day.
Two miles I had to walk along the fields
Before I reached my home. Magnificent
The morning was, a memorable pomp,
More glorious than I ever had beheld.
The Sea was laughing at a distance; all
The solid Mountains were as bright as clouds,
Grain-tinctured, drench'd in empyrean light;
And, in the meadows and the lower grounds,
Was all the sweetness of a common dawn,
Dews, vapours, and the melody of birds,
And Labourers going forth into the fields.
——Ah! need I say, dear Friend, that to the brim
My heart was full; I made no vows, but vows
Were then made for me; bond unknown to me
Was given, that I should be, else sinning greatly,
A dedicated Spirit. On I walk'd
In blessedness, which even yet remains.

(IV, 315–345)

On one level, at least, one could view this memory as a sort of anecdote, called forth in the poet's mind by association and framed on each side by general commentary about the course of his life. At bottom, however, the passage strives to accomplish more than it at first pretends, for the anecdote itself must create the transition from the offhanded introductory remark ("The memory of one particular hour / Doth here rise up against me") to the culminating statement ("On I walk'd / In blessedness, which even yet remains"). By the end of the passage, with its celebration of the ability of the past to project its powers into the present, Wordsworth has shifted context from casual reminiscence to religious vision.

In its whole rhetorical development the passage is typical of innumerable other "spots of time" scattered throughout *The Prelude*. Like the episode about the stolen boat in Book One ("One evening . . . I went alone into a Shepherd's Boat") it starts out by describing a tangible world of more or less ordinary things, in this instance a public celebration that occurs at regular intervals, almost like a ritual, to break the monotony of country routine. But its ritual quality ("a *festal* company") seems strictly secular in nature and only later in the description does the reader even become aware of the emotional effect it has upon Wordsworth ("Slight shocks of young love-liking . . .

/ That mounted up like joy into the head / And tingled through the veins"). The passion released here still remains essentially physical, though it points forward to the spiritual vision encompassed in the images of the sea and mountains, above all in the phrase "empyrean light." By the end of the passage everything that passes through the poet's view—fields, birds, laborers going off to their daily routine—all are endowed with a religious aura. The passage progresses, one might say, from "trivial pleasures" to "deeper passions" (both of these phrases are drawn from an introductory passage to this "spot of time"—ll. 305, 310); from a world of transitory things to intimations of a more eternal realm (which includes even the "Labourers going forth," who, in contrast to the dancers, are tied to the recurring cycle of nature); from the language of prose ("the memory of one particular hour") through a landscape appropriate to the short lyric ("and shuffling feet, / And glancing forms, and tapers glittering") to the Miltonic grandeur of the later lines ("Magnificent / The morning was, a memorable pomp"). In time the passage moves from a sense of great distance between Wordsworth's present state and the event he is depicting ("I *had pass'd* / The night in dancing") to a gradual apprehension of the oneness of past and present ("On I walk'd / In blessedness, which even yet remains"); moreover, what was trivial in the past—the surface gaiety of the dance—still retains its great distance in time, while the visionary experience of that night remains within him to dissolve the boundaries which the conceptualizing mind has created between present and past.

EMOTION REFRACTED

"In Wordsworth's most excited mood we have rather the reflexion of the flame than the authentic and derivative fire itself. Its heat and glare pass to us through some less pervious and colder lens."

Thus complained the *Gentleman's Magazine* in 1850, in a review of the newly published *Prelude.* The "fire itself," so conspicuously lacking in Wordsworth's poem, was amply to be found in Shelley's work, the reviewer assured his readers. To a mid-Victorian audience, accustomed as it was to a more heightened and direct expression of emotion than Wordsworth was willing to give, *The Prelude* must have seemed a relatively tame poem, too much akin, perhaps, to the contemplative verse of the eighteenth century to thrill the reader with the impassioned sweep he so much admired in *Prometheus Unbound.*

That "less pervious and colder lens" to which the reviewer objects might be described as Wordsworth's habit of approaching the more intense areas of his experience only by first insisting on their great distance in time. One might, in fact, speak of the "spot of time" as a distancing device, a way of portraying emotion by refracting it through experiences far distant from the present. The invariably prosaic openings of the "spots":

> When summer came
> It was the pastime of our afternoons
> (II, 55–56)

> Upon a small
> And rocky Island near, a fragment stood
> (Itself like a sea rock) of what had been
> A Romish Chapel
> (X, 518–21)

> One Christmas-time,
> The day before the Holidays began
> (XI, 345–6)

serve as a sort of lens through which the feelings about to be uncovered may be refracted and brought into open view. It is as though the poet were too reticent to release emotions directly, as though the distancing in time and the casualness of tone could make a deeply personal experience less overtly and embarrassingly personal; in our own age, indeed, the Victorian demand for the "flame itself" seems considerably more antiquated than Wordsworth's attempt to objectify feelings by refraction, a process which has something in common with such modern attempts to impersonalize emotions as we have come to characterize by the terms *persona, mask,* and *objective correlative.* Wordsworth, in fact, is sometimes at pains to separate his past self, which it is the object of the poem to explore, from the present self which speaks directly to the reader:

> So wide appears
> The vacancy between me and those days,
> Which yet have such self-presence in my mind

> That, sometimes, when I think of them, I seem
> Two consciousnesses, conscious of myself
> And of some other Being.
>
> (II, 28–33)

But if the spot of time in one sense serves to set emotion at an appropriately classical distance, in another sense it works to reawaken and set free long-since-forgotten feelings which, in turn, give new life and energy to the present. Or, to put it another way, the restrained classicism that characterizes the spot of time as a literary technique is counterbalanced through the claims which the spot of time makes for the meaningfulness of powerful feelings.

The ability of the retrospective process to help give vitality to the present through exploration of the past is at its most conspicuous, perhaps, in that spot of time in Book Eleven in which the poet describes his childhood visit to the scene where a murderer had once been executed. What is extraordinary about the passage is that Wordsworth does not explore merely a single past event, but that he moves through several separate points of time, each recalling the next by association and each, as it were, gathering up energy from the last. The passage starts out in the same casual way as the other spots of time:

> At a time
> When scarcely (I was then not six years old)
> My hand could hold a bridle, with proud hopes
> I mounted, and we rode towards the hills:
> We were a pair of Horsemen; honest James
> Was with me, my encourager and guide.
> We had not travell'd long, ere some mischance
> Disjoin'd me from my Comrade, and, through fear
> Dismounting, down the rough and stony Moor
> I led my Horse, and stumbling on, at length
> Came to a bottom, where in former times
> A Murderer had been hung in iron chains.
> The Gibbet-mast was moulder'd down, the bones
> And iron case were gone; but on the turf,
> Hard by, soon after that fell deed was wrought
> Some unknown hand had carved the Murderer's name.
>
> (XI, 279–94)

Thus far, we have no reason to expect anything more than straightforward narrative, something on the order of "Michael." The fussy preciseness with which Wordsworth interjects his age ("I was then not six years old"), the introduction of "honest James" as though he were already quite familiar to the reader, the painstakingness with which each of the poet's movements is recorded—all point to a prime concern with the things of this world. Only in the light of what follows would one look back on these details and speculate on more symbolic meanings: that the journey into the hills and into past time is as much a spiritual as a physical journey; and, moreover, that the story of the execution is weighted with some symbolic meaning (witness the "unknown hand," the "moulder'd' gibbet-mast", the phrase "in former times," whose plural form suggests a vast world of the past and points forward to the "times long past" a few lines later). The underlying significance of the incident becomes more evident in the lines that follow:

> The monumental writing was engraven
> In times long past, and still, from year to year,
> By superstition of the neighborhood,
> The grass is clear'd away; and to this hour
> The letters are all fresh and visible.
> Faltering, and ignorant where I was, at length
> I chanced to espy those characters inscribed
> On the green sod: forthwith I left the spot
> And, reascending the bare Common, saw
> A naked Pool that lay beneath the hills,
> The Beacon on the summit, and more near,
> A Girl who bore a Pitcher on her head
> And seem'd with difficult steps to force her way
> Against the blowing wind. It was, in truth,
> An ordinary sight; but I should need
> Colours and words that are unknown to man
> To paint the visionary dreariness
> Which, while I look'd all round for my lost Guide,
> Did at that time invest the naked Pool,
> The Beacon on the lonely Eminence,
> The Woman, and her garments vex'd and toss'd
> By the strong wind.
>
> (XI, 295–316)

Thus far we are aware of three separate points of time: the present, from which Wordsworth looks back to his childhood and from which, in turn, a new perspective is introduced upon far earlier times. The "monumental" quality of the carved letters; the ritual of clearing away the grass (in citing local superstitions Wordsworth anticipates a device employed by novelists like Hawthorne to hint at deeper meanings which they neither wish to verify nor make too explicit); the everlasting "freshness" of the letters (contrasting with the "moulder'd gibbet-mast," as if to indicate the vitality latent in the seemingly dead past)—all, by the very intensity they call forth, prepare the ground (literally even) for the vision that follows. At this point the poet confronts the letters directly and, as though instinctively gathering up the energies latent within the scene, begins a new "journey," upward, to a point from which he can view the three objects—the pool, the beacon, the girl—which form the center of the vision. Yet these objects, awesome as they seem to the poet, are presented on a naturalistic level—an "ordinary sight," as Wordsworth at first puts it—and are not drawn from any recognizable tradition of symbols. If one encountered such images in the work of a conscious symbolist such as Blake or Shelley one would feel impelled to seek out a symbolic meaning for each of them. But in the present context the three images seem less significant for the individual meanings which we can assign to them than for the total effect which they produce. Through the animating medium of the wind they are fused together into a single momentous vision, which in its bleakness and fierceness seems to suggest the precariousness of human endeavor in the face of larger forces (the girl balancing the pitcher on her head is still another of Wordsworth's figures of endurance, like Margaret in *The Ruined Cottage*). Beyond that, the wind, with all the brute power which it symbolizes, sets into motion a new, even more intense movement of thought. As though having gathered something of its power within himself, Wordsworth moves forward once more to the present time in order to contemplate the past vision in still further perspective. Once again, in the final lines quoted, the three objects reappear, but the tone with which they are listed is more formal, almost declamatory, as if to indicate the far greater intensity with which they are now charged in his mind.

Thus far the incident is complete as it was first written, probably in 1798. But Wordsworth added still a new perspective in time in 1804, during the later stages of the poem's composition:

When, in a blessed season
With those two dear Ones, to my heart so dear,
When in the blessed time of early love,
Long afterwards, I roam'd about
In daily presence of this very scene,
Upon the naked pool and dreary crags,
And on the melancholy Beacon, fell
The spirit of pleasure and youth's golden gleam;
And think ye not with radiance more divine
From these remembrances, and from the power
They left behind? So feeling comes in aid
Of feeling, and diversity of strength
Attends us, if but once we have been strong.
Oh! mystery of Man, from what a depth
Proceed thy honours! I am lost, but see
In simple childhood something of the base
On which thy greatness stands, but this I feel,
That from thyself it is that thou must give
Else never canst receive. The days gone by
Come back upon me from the dawn almost
Of life: the hiding-places of my power
Seem open; I approach, and then they close;
I see by glimpses now; when age comes on,
May scarcely see at all, and I would give,
While yet we may, as far as words can give,
A substance and a life to what I feel:
I would enshrine the spirit of the past
For future restoration.

(XI, 316–43)

In its final development the memory of this dreary scene is refracted through still another memory, this one benign with "the spirit of pleasure and youth's golden gleam." To put it another way, the memory of early love works to transform the "visionary dreariness" of the earlier memory into a more benign, though no less forceful power. If I may take up once more the metaphor with which I started, the energies latent in Wordsworth's memories are like rays of light that pass through a prism and reveal constantly new possibilities of color to the observing eye. But analogies will go only a short way to illuminate a process which remains so largely implicit in the text.

Wordsworth himself describes the process with deliberate imprecision: "So feeling comes in aid / Of feeling." Thus, while reflecting in 1798 upon the meaning of his earliest memories, he cites a particular incident which occurred when he was six; reflection upon this incident, in turn, opens up a more distant and impersonal past, the time of the murderer's execution ("Times long past"); and this memory, in turn, recalls another, much later personal memory, from his eighteenth or nineteenth year. But if this process, on one level, consists of a simple, though non-chronological, line of mental associations, on another level it takes the form of a mysterious and complex transfer of power, both backward and forward, from one period of time to another: the memory of young love, though recalled by the frightening earlier childhood memory, sets this earlier memory into a new, more benign perspective and thus transforms it, while the combined effect of these memories will project into the future—a future well beyond the time of writing—to comfort the aging poet and, beyond that, through the "substance" and "life" with which they have been endowed in his poetry, to exert their effect upon readers in an even more distant future. And yet the whole process— down to the climactic statement, "Oh! mystery of Man, from what a depth / Proceed thy honours!"—seems to follow so naturally from the incident narrated off-handedly at the beginning that the reader is scarcely aware of the complexity of the thought structure into which he has been led.

In a discussion of another spot of time—the one directly following, of the poet waiting in the storm at Christmastime for the horses to fetch him home—A. C. Bradley long ago remarked, "Everything here is natural, but everything is apocalyptic. And we happen to know why. Wordsworth is describing the scene in the light of memory." The writer who sets out to recapture the past can thus do two things simultaneously: on the pretext of telling the reader something about himself he can uncover an objective, tangible world and at the same time he can cast a mythical aura about it. He can reveal it in all its concrete fullness and he can use it as a symbol of still another world behind it. He can be both realist and symbolist at once.

One could speculate that Wordsworth's decision to make the recovery of his own past the subject of *The Prelude* forced him to develop that peculiar approach to metaphor which, [elsewhere], I described in my discussion of his "images of interaction." Facing the dual task of retelling past events and at the same time convincing the reader of their significance, he developed a way of doing both at once: reality became symbol, concrete detail became abstraction, description became assertion, tenor and vehicle became indistinguishable. What separates *The Prelude* at once from the poems of personal or pseudo-personal reminiscence of the late eighteenth century is the fact that the individual memories and the poet's discursive comments upon them are no longer scattered about, tied to one another only by association, but rather that Wordsworth has worked out a new rhetorical form, a new genre, in fact, to fuse together concrete perception and a statement of its significance, and beyond that to make poetry assert and celebrate at the same time it describes and analyzes. Earl R. Wasserman, in *The Subtler Language*, his recent attempt to define the essential difference between eighteenth- and nineteenth-century poetry, described the task of the romantic poets in the following terms:

> Largely deprived of *topoi* rich in publicly accessible values and cut off from the older conceptions of world-orders, they [the poets of the early nineteenth century] were compelled to cultivate fresh values in the objects of experience and to organize these values into a special structure within the poem so as to avail themselves of the expressive powers of a revivified vocabulary and a new syntactical system. It is, therefore, not merely in the overt statements, often disarmingly simple, but especially in the inner subtleties of their language—in the recurrences and transformations of images, in what superficially might seem only a convenient and otherwise purposeless turn of phrase, for example—that we must seek the articulation of a modern poem's fullest meaning.

The spot of time, one might say, is that "special structure" which Wordsworth organized out of the objects of his personal experience—a structure, moreover, which articulates its meanings not primarily through traditional figures of speech appealing to an outward frame of reference, but by creating its own rhetoric—for instance, through the use of different intensities of tone at each of the three times the images of the pool, the beacon, and the girl with the pitcher appear—which in turn evolves its own inner frame of reference.

The poetic values represented by the spot of time, rooted as they are in concrete experience, have become so central a part of modern poetic tradition that, despite the obvious differences between the language of modern poetry and Wordsworth's "rhetoric of interaction," we often tend to read *The Prelude* piecemeal for its spots of time. "*The Prelude* is at the center of our experience of Wordsworth; at the center of our experience of *The Prelude* are those 'spots of time' where Wordsworth is endeavoring to express key moments in the history of his imagination"—thus begins a recent psychological interpretation of these passages. (Jonathan Bishop, "Wordsworth and the 'Spots of Time,' " *ELH* 26 (1959):45). To the extent that the spots of time attempt to fragmentize experience or to work toward the evocation of pure states of being—the "trances of thought and mountings of the mind" to which Wordsworth refers at the opening of the poem—they point forward to that conception of what was properly poetic which, in the century after *The Prelude*, was increasingly to claim exclusive domain over the province of poetry. If we have been inclined, perhaps, to lift the spots of time too readily out of their larger context, this is not merely a sign of their special modernity, but also, as I argued [elsewhere], of the fact that we have lost the art of reading long poems.

Wordsworth's Long Journey Home

M. H. Abrams

THE IDEA OF THE PRELUDE

In this era of constant and drastic experimentation with literary materials and forms, it is easy to overlook the radical novelty of *The Prelude* when it was completed in 1805. The poem amply justified Wordsworth's claim to have demonstrated original genius, which he defined as "the introduction of a new element into the intellectual universe" of which the "infallible sign is the widening the sphere of human sensibility."

The Prelude is a fully developed poetic equivalent of two portentous innovations in prose fiction, of which the earliest examples had appeared in Germany only a decade or so before Wordsworth began writing his poem: the *Bildungsroman* (Wordsworth called *The Prelude* a poem on "the growth of my own mind") and the *Künstlerroman* (Wordsworth also spoke of it as "a poem on my own poetical education," and it far surpassed all German examples in the detail with which his "history," as he said, was specifically "of a *Poet's* mind"). The whole poem is written as a sustained address to Coleridge—"I speak bare truth / As if alone to thee in private talk" (X, 372–3); Coleridge, however, is an auditor *in absentia*, and the solitary author often supplements this form with an interior monologue, or else carries on an extended colloquy with the landscape in which the interlocutors are "my mind" and "the speaking face of earth and

From *Natural Supernaturalism*. © 1971 by W. W. Norton & Co. Originally entitled "The Idea of *The Prelude*" and "William Wordsworth: The Long Journey Home."

heaven" (V, 11–12). [References are to 1805 version unless otherwise noted.] The construction of *The Prelude* is radically achronological, starting not at the beginning, but at the end—during Wordsworth's walk to "the Vale that I had chosen" (I, 100), which telescopes the circumstances of two or more occasions but refers primarily to his walk to the Vale of Grasmere, that "hermitage" (I, 115) where he has taken up residence at that stage of his life with which the poem concludes. During this walk an outer breeze, "the sweet breath of Heaven," evokes within the poet "a corresponding mild creative breeze," a prophetic *spiritus* or inspiration which assures him of his poetic mission and, though it is fitful, eventually leads to his undertaking *The Prelude* itself; in the course of the poem, at times of imaginative dryness, the revivifying wind recurs in the role of a poetic leitmotif.

Wordsworth does not tell his life as a simple narrative in past time but as the present remembrance of things past, in which forms and sensations "throw back our life" (I, 660–1) and evoke the former self which coexists with the altered present self in a multiple awareness that Wordsworth calls "two consciousnesses." There is a wide "vacancy" between the I now and the I then,

> Which yet have such self-presence in my mind
> That, sometimes, when I think of them, I seem
> Two consciousnesses, conscious of myself
> And of some other Being.   (II, 27–33)

The poet is aware of the near impossibility of disengaging "the naked recollection of that time" from the intrusions of "after-meditation" (III, 644–8). In a fine and subtle figure for the interdiffusion of the two consciousnesses, he describes himself as one bending from a drifting boat on a still water, perplexed to distinguish actual objects at the bottom of the lake from surface reflections of the environing scene, from the tricks and refractions of the water currents, and from his own intrusive but inescapable image (that is, his present awareness). Thus "incumbent o'er the surface of past time" the poet, seeking the elements of continuity between his two disparate selves, conducts a persistent exploration of the nature and significance of memory, of his power to sustain freshness of sensation and his "first creative sensibility" against the deadening effect of habit and analysis, and of manifestations of the enduring and the eternal within the realm of change and time. Only intermittently does the narrative order coincide with the order of actual occurrence. Instead Wordsworth proceeds by sometimes bewildering ellipses, fusions, and as he says, "motions retrograde" in time (IX, 8).

Scholars have long been aware that it is perilous to rely on the factual validity of *The Prelude*, and in consequence Wordsworth has been charged with intellectual uncertainty, artistic ineptitude, bad memory, or even bad faith. The poem has suffered because we know so much about the process of its composition between 1798 and 1805—its evolution from a constituent part to a "tail-piece" to a "portico" of *The Recluse*, and Wordsworth's late decision to add to the beginning and end of the poem the excluded middle: his experiences in London and in France. A work is to be judged, however, as a finished and free-standing product; and in *The Prelude* as it emerged after six years of working and reworking, the major alterations and dislocations of the events of Wordsworth's life are imposed deliberately, in order that the design inherent in that life, which has become apparent only to his mature awareness, may stand revealed as a principle which was invisibly operative from the beginning. A supervising idea, in other words, controls Wordsworth's account and shapes it into a structure in which the protagonist is put forward as one who has been elected to play a special role in a providential plot. As Wordsworth said in the opening passage, which represents him after he has reached maturity: in response to the quickening outer breeze

> to the open fields I told
> A prophecy: poetic numbers came
> Spontaneously, and cloth'd in priestly robe
> My spirit, thus singled out, as it might seem
> For holy services.
>
> (I, 59–63)

Hence in this history of a poet's mind the poet is indeed the "transitory Being," William Wordsworth, but he is also the exemplary poet-prophet who has been singled out, in a time "of hopes o'er-thrown . . . of dereliction and dismay," to bring mankind tidings of comfort and joy; as Wordsworth put it in one version of the Prospectus,

> that my verse may live and be
> Even as a light hung up in heaven to chear
> Mankind in times to come.

The spaciousness of his chosen form allows Wordsworth to introduce some of the clutter and contingency of ordinary experience. In accordance with his controlling idea, however, he selects for extended treatment only those of his actions and experiences which are significant for his evolution toward an inherent end, and organizes his life around an event which he regards as the spiritual crisis not of himself only, but of his generation: that shattering of the fierce loyalties and inordinate hopes for mankind which the liberal English—and European—intellectuals had invested in the French Revolution.

> Not in my single self alone I found,
> But in the minds of all ingenuous Youth,
> Change and subversion from this hour.
> (X, 232–4)

The Prelude, correspondingly, is ordered in three stages. There is a process of mental development which, although at times suspended, remains a continuum; this process is violently broken by a crisis of apathy and despair; but the mind then recovers an integrity which, despite admitted losses, is represented as a level higher than the initial unity, in that the mature mind possesses powers, together with an added range, depth, and sensitivity of awareness, which are the products of the critical experiences it has undergone. The discovery of this fact resolves a central problem which has been implicit throughout *The Prelude*—the problem of how to justify the human experience of pain and loss and suffering; he is now able to recognize that his life is "in the end / All gratulant if rightly understood" (XIII, 384–5).

The narrative is punctuated with recurrent illuminations, or "spots of time," and is climaxed by two major revelations. The first of these is Wordsworth's discovery of precisely what he has been born to be and to do. At Cambridge he had reached a stage of life, "an eminence," in which he had felt that he was "a chosen Son" (III, 82 ff., 169), and on a walk home from a dance during a summer dawn he had experienced an illumination that he should be, "else sinning greatly, / A dedicated Spirit" (IV, 343–4); but for what chosen, or to what dedicated, had not been specified. Now, however, the recovery from the crisis of despair after his commitment to the French Revolution comprises the insight that his destiny is not one of engagement with what is blazoned "with the pompous names / Of power and action" in "the stir / And tumult of the world," but one of withdrawal from the world of action so that he may meditate in solitude: his role in life requires not involvement, but detachment. And that role is to be one of the "Poets, even as Prophets," each of whom is endowed with the power "to perceive / Something unseen before," and so to write a new kind of poetry in a new poetic style. "Of these, said I, shall be my Song; of these... / Will I record the praises": the ordinary world of lowly, suffering men and of commonplace or trivial things transformed into "a new world... fit / To be transmitted," of dignity, love, and heroic grandeur (XII, 220–379). Wordsworth's crisis, then, involved what we now call a crisis of identity, which was resolved in the discovery of "my office upon earth" (X, 921). And since the specification of this office entails the definition, in the twelfth book, of the particular innovations in poetic subjects, style, and values toward which his life had been implicitly oriented, *The Prelude* is a poem which incorporates the discovery of its own *ars poetica*.

His second revelation he achieves on a mountaintop. The occasion is the ascent of Mount Snowdon, which Wordsworth, in accordance with his controlling idea, excerpts from its chronological position in his life in 1791, before the crucial experience of France, and describes in the concluding book of *The Prelude*. As he breaks through the cover of clouds the light of the moon "upon the turf / Fell like a flash," and he sees the total scene as "the perfect image of a mighty Mind" in its free and continuously creative reciprocation with its milieu, "Willing to work and to be wrought upon" and so to "create / A like existence" (XIII, 36–119). What has been revealed to Wordsworth in this symbolic landscape is the grand locus of *The Recluse* which he announced in the Prospectus, "The Mind of Man— / My haunt, and the main region of my song," as well as the "high argument" of that poem, the union between the mind and the external world and the resulting "creation... which they with blended might / Accomplish." The event which Wordsworth selects for the climactic revelation in *The Prelude*, then, is precisely the moment of the achievement of "this Vision" by "the transitory Being" whose life he had, in the Prospectus, undertaken to describe as an integral part of *The Recluse*.

In the course of *The Prelude* Wordsworth repeatedly drops the clue that his work has been designed to round back to its point of departure. "Not with these began / Our Song, and not with these our Song must end," he had cried after the crisis of France, invoking the "breezes and soft airs" that had blown in the "glad preamble" to his poem (XI, 1 ff. and VII, 1 ff.). As he nears the end of the song, he says that his self-discovery constitutes a religious conclusion ("The rapture of the Hallelujah sent / From all that breathes and is") which is at the same time, as he had planned from the outset, an artistic beginning:

> And now, O Friend; this history is brought
> To its appointed close: the discipline
> And consummation of the Poet's mind.
>   . . . we have reach'd
> The time (which was our object from the first)
> When we may, not presumptuously, I hope,
> Suppose my powers so far confirmed, and such
> My knowledge, as to make me capable
> Of building up a work that should endure.
> (XIII, 261–78)

That work, of course, is *The Recluse*, for which *The Prelude* was designed to serve as "portico . . . part of the same building." *The Prelude*, then, is an involuted poem which is about its own genesis— a prelude to itself. Its structural end is its own beginning; and its temporal beginning, as I have pointed out, is Wordsworth's entrance upon the stage of his life at which it ends. The conclusion goes on to specify the circular shape of the whole. Wordsworth there asks Coleridge to "Call back to mind / The mood in which this Poem was begun." At that time,

>   I rose
> As if on wings, and saw beneath me stretch'd
> Vast prospect of the world which I had been
> And was; and hence this Song, which like a lark
> I have protracted.
> (XIII, 370–81)

This song, describing the prospect of his life which had been made visible to him at the opening of *The Prelude*, is *The Prelude* whose composition he is even now concluding. . . .

THE LONG JOURNEY HOME

I have "never read a word of German metaphysics, thank Heaven!" Wordsworth wrote to Henry Crabb Robinson. This claim is no doubt the literal truth; yet as Robinson several times remarked, Wordsworth's thinking frequently parallels that of his philosophical German contemporaries. Prominent in Wordsworth, for example, is his version of the great commonplace of the age: unity with himself and his world is the primal and normative state of man, of which the sign is a fullness of shared life and the condition of joy; analytic thought divides the mind from nature and object from object, and this division, if absolute, kills the object it severs and threatens with spiritual death the mind from which it has been severed. In the second book of *The Prelude* Wordsworth praises Coleridge as one to whom "the unity of all has been reveal'd," and who is therefore free from the slavery "Of that false secondary power, by which / In weakness, we create distinctions" that we mistake for real divisions. He goes on to oppose to "analytic industry" his own "observations of affinities / In objects where no brotherhood exists / To common minds," with the eventual result that "in all things / I saw one life, and felt that it was joy." In a manuscript passage he adds that "by such communion" he was "early taught" that the separate "forms and images" evident to passive perception, as well as the divisive processes of active "thought / Prospectiveness, intelligence or will," seem but "relapses"—that is, a falling away—from the undifferentiated oneness of self with nature, and of both these with God:

> Such consciousnesses seemed but accidents
> Relapses from the one interior life
> Which is in all things, from that unity
> In which all beings live with God, are lost
> In god and nature, in one mighty whole
> As undistinguishable as the cloudless east
> At noon is from the cloudless west when all
> The hemisphere is one cerulean blue.

Some two years earlier, in a passage intended for *The Ruined Cottage*, Wordsworth's Pedlar had denounced the false kind of "science" which, instead of serving "the cause / Of order and distinctness" (that is, by distinction without division), murders, by disconnecting, both the objects seen and the self that sees:

> For was it meant
> That we should pore, and dwindle as we pore . . .
> On solitary objects, still beheld

> In disconnection dead and spiritless
> And still dividing and dividing still,
> Break down all grandeur...
>   waging thus
> An impious warfare with the very life
> Of our own souls?

"Let us rise," he cries, "From this oblivious sleep"—patently this is the "sleep of Death" from which Wordsworth undertook to waken "the sensual" in his Prospectus—and reunite the severed parts in a resurrective interchange in which (as Coleridge was to phrase it in his *Dejection*) the life of all things will be the eddying of our living soul:

>   Thus disciplined
> All things shall live in us and we shall live
> In all things that surround us. . . .
> For thus the senses and the intellect
> Shall each to each supply a mutual aid...
> And forms and feelings acting thus, and thus
> Reacting, they shall each acquire
> A living spirit and a character
> Till then unfelt.

In "The Fountain" (1799) Wordsworth gave to the old man Matthew a memorable statement about the unhappy consciousness of self-divided and knowingly mortal man and the happy self-unity of creatures who act by instinct, and without memory or anticipation:

> The Blackbird amid leafy trees,
> The lark above the hill,
> Let loose their carols when they please,
> Are quiet when they will.
>
> With Nature never do *they* wage
> A foolish strife; they see
> A happy youth, and their old age
> Is beautiful and free.

Like Schiller and Coleridge, Wordsworth here expresses, through the medium of an invented character, man's discontent with being human and civilized. When he speaks in his own person, however,

Wordsworth conceives the mature mind as an integrity of disparate elements which is the product of a growth that necessarily involves self-division and conflict. His general norm is a unity which retains individual identity, and his particular ideal of life (as John Jones has put it) is to sustain solitude in relationship. Thus Wordsworth proclaimed, in one version of his Prospectus,

> Of the individual mind that keeps its own
> Inviolate retirement, and consists
> With being limitless, the one great Life
> I sing.

The great distinction of Wordsworth's *Prelude* in its age is that it is not (as Coleridge tried to make it) a philosophical poem, nor an extended cosmic myth, nor a symbolic or allegorical fable, but the presentation of a particular person, unique yet humanly representative, as he develops from infancy to maturity through his evolving experience with his natural environment, with other men, and with the great public events of his time. Wordsworth nevertheless claimed that his poetry possessed a systematic intellectual ground; as he said of *The Recluse* of which *The Prelude* was a part, while "it is not the Author's intention formally to announce a system . . . the Reader will have no difficulty in extracting the system for himself." His confidence in the reader is perhaps excessive; but our present point of vantage enables us to discern in *The Prelude* a coherent understructure of ideas and a sustained evolution of images which mark its consonance with the thought and design of a number of other, and very diverse, Romantic works of literature and philosophy.

I remarked [elsewhere] that, on one recurrent level of narrative, Wordsworth undertakes to represent the growth of a poet's mind— just as German philosophers undertook to construct the development of generic and individual consciousness—within the limits of a two-term scheme of reference: the interactions between subject and object, mind and nature. Unlike the German Idealists, however, Wordsworth does not posit an initial One, or absolute, which subdivides into the knowing mind and the object known, but instead begins, as he says in the Prospectus, with a "Mind" which is fitted to "the external World" and an "external World" which is "fitted to the Mind." In the early books of *The Prelude* he sets out to show the slow and complex workings of "those first-born affinities that fit / Our new existence to existing things" (I, 582–3), in the process by which the mind of the child, through the mediation of its senses, grows into community with its environing world. Natural objects enter, flow, are received, and sink down into the mind, while the mind dwells in, feeds on, drinks, holds intercourse with, and weaves, intertwines, fastens, and binds itself to external objects, until the two integrate as one. These are Wordsworth's recurrent metaphors, the essential lexicon he developed to enable him to say, about the development of man's cognitive and emotional involvement with the milieu into which he is born, what had never been explicitly said before, and with a subtlety that has not been exceeded since. In the crowning figure of this metaphoric complex the babe, in the security of his mother's arms, evolves into awareness of a world which is so thoroughly humanized that the pull of gravity is experienced as a familial relationship. "In one beloved presence,"

> there exists
> A virtue which irradiates and exalts
> All objects through all intercourse of sense.
> No outcast he, bewilder'd and depress'd;
> Along his infant veins are interfus'd
> The gravitation and filial bond
> Of nature, that connect him with the world.
> (II, 255–64)

The dynamic element in the growth of the mind in nature is a play of polarities which is not, in Wordsworth, a systematic dialectic, but instead operates, as Charles J. Smith has said, as "a very strong habit of thinking in terms of paired opposites or contrarities. Everywhere in nature, in individual man and in society, [Wordsworth] saw a constant interplay of opposing forces." Chief among the contraries in nature, we already know, are those which Wordsworth introduces in his opening lines on his interaction with the natural scene: "I grew up / Foster'd alike by beauty and by fear" (I, 305–6). Related to this opposition between incitation by beauty and discipline by terror are other contraries which constitute the poles between which flow the forces of "this active universe." "Calmness" and "emotion," "peace and excitation," "stillness" and "energy"—"these two attributes / Are sister horns that constitute her strength."

In Wordsworth's account his community with the natural milieu precedes, and is instrumental to, his development of a community with other men: "Love of Nature" leads to "Love of

Mankind." The integrity of mind that he has achieved receives its first serious test in London, both on his first brief visit, when he "felt in heart and soul the shock / Of the huge town's first presence" (1850; VII, 66–7), and during the period of his later residence there. The "blank confusion" of the metropolis terrified Wordsworth by a double threat to his sense of individuation-in-unity: by fragmenting community into an anarchy of unrelated parts, and by assimilating the parts into a homogeneity in which no individuality survives,

> melted and reduced
> To one identity, by differences
> That have no law, no meaning, and no end.

But the strength of the integral fabric of consciousness wrought by his earlier education in nature enabled him to manage even this "unmanageable sight," as one who "sees the parts / As parts, but with a feeling of the whole." "The forms / Perennial of the ancient hills," changeless in "the changeful language of their countenances," had provided him with a model for reconciling "multitude, / With order and relation"; and now "the Spirit of Nature" remained "present as a habit," and served to diffuse through

> the press
> Of self-destroying, transitory things
> Composure and ennobling harmony.
> (VII, 695–740)

This development "Of intellectual power, from stage to stage/ Advancing, hand in hand with love and joy, / And of imagination," is shattered by the "over-pressure of the times / And their disastrous issues" (XI, 42–48). Wordsworth describes the process of his breakdown as the cumulative fragmentation and conflict of once integral elements. He turned to abstract reason to furnish support for his failing hopes, but this was in effect to foster a divisive inner "war against myself," in the attempt "to cut off my heart / From all the sources of her former strength" and to unsoul by logic "those mysteries of passion which have made... / One brotherhood of the human race" (XI, 74–88). Analytic reason divides, but it cannot reunify, for it sets up the kind of inert contraries which cannot be resolved: "Sick, wearied out with contrarieties," I "Yielded up moral questions in despair. / This was the crisis of that strong disease" (1850; XI, 304–6). At the same time the "life of nature," which should have sustained and guided him, had itself succumbed to the same work of "logic and minute analysis." Hitherto he had rejoiced in its passion and its life, in which he had participated because he had confronted nature with unified and cooperative faculties and feelings,

> now all eye
> And now all ear; but ever with the heart
> Employ'd, and the majestic intellect.

But inner division became inner conflict and resulted in a state in which "the eye was master of the heart" and "often held my mind in absolute dominion" (XI, 96–180). The consequence of such division between mind and nature, and the resulting enslavement of the mind by "the laws of vulgar sense," was to destroy "a world of life" and transform it into "a universe of death" (XIII, 102–3, 138–41).

The poet's recovery, correspondingly, is represented as a gradual reintegration of all that had been divided: his faculties, senses, and feelings, his past and present self, and his mind and outer nature. My sister, Wordsworth says, "Maintained for me a saving intercourse / With my true self," while "Nature's self . . . led me back" to the earlier "counsels between head and heart" (1850; XI, 335–54); the persistence in memory of "spots of time" helped him to reestablish continuity between the self that he is and the self that he was; and he finally reachieved the integrity of being that he had lost, although now on a level of consciousness which preserved the critical experiences through which he had passed.

> Behold me then
> Once more in Nature's presence, thus restored
> Or otherwise, and strengthened once again
> (With memory left of what had been escaped).

It is time to notice that Wordsworth's account of unity achieved, lost, and regained is held together, as various critics have remarked, by the recurrent image of a journey: like a number of works by his contemporaries, Wordsworth's "poem on my own poetical education" converts the wayfaring Christian of the Augustinian spiritual journey into the self-formative traveler of the Romantic educational journey. The poem in fact opens, as Elizabeth Sewell has said, "with the poet in a prospect of wide landscape and open sky," on a literal walk which serves as "the great over-all poetic figure or trope of a journey which he is about to undertake." In the course of this episode the aimless wanderer becomes "as a Pilgrim resolute" who takes "the road that pointed toward the chosen Vale," and at the end of the first book the road translates itself into the metaphorical way of his life's pilgrimage:

> Forthwith shall be brought down
> Through later years the story of my life.
> The road lies plain before me.
> (1850; I, 91–93, 638–40)

The Prelude is replete with "the Wanderers of the Earth," and after the period of childhood, its chief episodes are Wordsworth's own wanderings through the English countryside, the Alps, Italy, France, and Wales—literal journeys through actual places which modulate easily into symbolic landscapes traversed by a metaphorical wayfarer. This organizing figure works in two dimensions. In one of these, *The Prelude* represents the life which the poet narrates as a self-educative journey, "from stage to stage / Advancing," in which his early development had been "progress on the self-same path," the crisis following the French Revolution had been "a stride at once / Into another region," and the terminus was his achievement of maturity in "the discipline / And consummation of the Poet's mind." In the second application, the poet repeatedly figures his own imaginative enterprise, the act of composing *The Prelude* itself, as a perilous quest through the uncharted regions of his own mind.

At times the vehicle for this latter poetic journey is a voyage at sea, connoting the wanderings of Odysseus in his search for home:

> What avail'd,
> When Spells forbade the Voyager to land,
> The fragrance which did ever and anon
> Give notice of the Shore? . . .
> My business was upon the barren sea
> My errand was to sail to other coasts.

Elsewhere Wordsworth's implied parallel is to Dante, who "Nell mezzo del cammin di nostra vita" had been granted a visionary journey, with a relay of guides, through hell and the earthly paradise to heaven:

> A Traveller I am,
> And all my Tale is of myself; even so,
> So be it, if the pure in heart delight
> To follow me; and Thou, O honor'd Friend!
> Who in my thoughts art ever at my side,
> Uphold, as heretofore, my fainting steps.
>
> (III, 196–201)

At the beginning of the ninth book, "as a traveller, who has gained the brow / Of some aerial Down" and "is tempted to review / The region left behind him," Wordsworth turns back to his earlier youth, before he moves reluctantly on into the discordant "argument" that begins with his residence in France—"Oh, how much unlike the past!" The eleventh book, narrating the process of Wordsworth's recovery, opens in a parallel to Milton's description of his epic journey back from hell to the realms of light (XI, 1–7; see *Paradise Lost*, III, 13–20). And through all these regions the imagined presence of Coleridge serves both as auditor and guide, heartening the exhausted poet in his pilgrimage and quest:

> Thou wilt not languish here, O Friend, for whom
> I travel in these dim uncertain ways
> Thou wilt assist me as a Pilgrim gone
> In quest of highest truth.
>
> (XI, 390–3)

The last book of *The Prelude*, in symmetry with its first book, also opens with a literal walk which translates itself into a metaphor for the climactic stage both of the journey of life and of the imaginative journey which is the poem itself. This time the walk is not a movement along an open plain but the ascent of a mountain, the traditional place for definitive visions since Moses had climbed Mount Sinai. As in Hegel's *Phenomenology* the spirit, at the close of its educational journey, recognizes itself in its other, so Wordsworth's mind, confronting nature, discovers itself in its own perfected powers:

> A meditation rose in me that night
> Upon the lonely Mountain . . .
>   and it appear'd to me
> The perfect image of a mighty Mind.

In the earliest stage of its development Wordsworth's "Babe, / Nurs'd in his Mother's arms" had not only acquired "The gravitation and the filial bond ... that connect him with the world," but had also, as "inmate of this *active* universe," established the beginnings of the reciprocative power by which

> his mind ...
> Creates, creator and receiver both,
> Working but in alliance with the works
> Which it beholds.—Such, verily, is the first
> Poetic spirit of our human life.
>
> (II, 265–76)

On Mount Snowdon, in an evident parallel and complement to this early passage, his mind recognizes, in that image of itself "which Nature thus / Thrusts forth upon the senses" the same power, which has now developed into "the fulness of its strength." As mist and moonlight transform the natural scene, so higher minds by a similar "Power"

> can send abroad
> Like transformation, for themselves create
> A like existence, and, whene'er it is
> Created for them, catch it by an instinct ...
> Willing to work and to be wrought upon

by the works which they behold. An essential alteration, however, is that the mature poetic mind, whose infant perception had been a state of undifferentiated consciousness, has acquired self-consciousness, and is able to sustain the sense of its own identity as an individuation-in-unison with the objects it perceives. In Wordsworth's terse rendering,

> hence the highest bliss
> That can be known is theirs, the consciousness
> Of whom they are habitually infused
> Through every image, and through every thought,
> And all impressions.
>
> (XIII, 84–111)

I have already remarked ... that *The Prelude* has a circular organization. This circularity of its form, we now see, reflects the circularity of its subject matter. In the opening passage of *The Prelude* the narrator is confirmed in his vocation as a poet-prophet and, in response to an impulse from the autumnal wood, chooses as his goal "a known Vale, whither my feet should turn," in the assurance "of some work of glory there forthwith to be begun." "Keen as a Truant or a Fugitive, / But as a Pilgrim resolute," and also (in a complementary pedestrian metaphor) "like a home-bound labourer," he then pursued his way until a three days' walk "brought me to my hermitage" (1850; I, 71–80, 90–107). At the end of *The Prelude* Wordsworth, having taken up his "permanent abode" (XIII, 338) in this hermitage, calls "back to mind" the occasion of its beginning. But *The Prelude* has a complex function, for it is designed not only as a poem in itself, but also as a "portico" to *The Recluse*. The spiritual journey thus circles back at its conclusion to the literal journey with which it had originated; but his beginning at once turns over into the opening book of Wordsworth's "work of glory," *The Recluse* proper, which describes his way of life in the chosen vale. Only now does he identify the aspect of the vale which had all along made it the goal of his tortuous literal, spiritual, and poetic journey. That goal, as in all the ancient genre of the circuitous pilgrimage, is home— "Home at Grasmere."

The initial passage of "Home at Grasmere" makes it clear that the place to which the poet has returned is not his literal home but one which, on his first overview of the "Vale below" when, solitary, he had chanced across it as "a roving School-boy," he had recognized to be his spiritual home. "Perfect was the Spot . . . stirring to the Spirit"; and he had immediately felt that "here / Must be his Home, this Valley be his World." Throughout his youth the vale had lingered in memory, "shedding upon joy / A brighter joy," and now the home of his imagining has become his actual home (the word reverberates through the opening passage):

> And now 'tis mine, perchance for life, dear Vale,
> Beloved Grasmere (let the Wandering Streams
> Take up, the cloud-capt hills repeat, the Name),
> One of thy lowly Dwellings is my Home.

The place in which, "on Nature's invitation" (line 71), Wordsworth's literal and metaphoric wanderings have terminated is identified, after the venerable formula, as a home which is also a recovered paradise. In his Pisgah-sight of it as a schoolboy he had looked upon it as a "paradise before him" (line 14); and it remains, after he takes up his abode in it, an "earthly counterpart" of heaven (line 642), which he describes in terms echoing Milton's description of the Gar-

den of Eden, and in which Wordsworth and Dorothy, "A solitary
pair" (line 255) are somewhat incongruously the Adam and Eve. The
journey to this ultimate stage has taken him through "the realities
of life so cold," but this had been a fortunate fall into experience,
for "the cost" of what he has lost from the earlier stage of his life is
greatly outweighed by "what I keep, have gain'd / Shall gain," so
that

> in my day of Childhood I was less
> The mind of Nature, less, take all in all,
> Whatever may be lost, than I am now.

For him, man's ancient dream of felicity has been brought down
from a transcendent heaven and located in this very world—

> the distant thought
> Is fetch'd out of the heaven in which it was.
> The unappropriated bliss hath found
> An owner, and that owner I am he.
> The Lord of this enjoyment is on Earth
> And in my breast.

Here he dwells, therefore, as a second and more fortunate Adam,
because unlike his predecessor he possesses an Eden which has been
gained:

> The boon is absolute; surpassing grace
> To me hath been vouchsafed; among the bowers
> Of blissful Eden this was neither given,
> Nor could be given, possession of the good
> Which had been sighed for, ancient thought fulfilled
> And dear Imaginations realized
> Up to their highest measure, yea and more.

As in comparable passages in Hölderlin and Novalis (in Blake the
parallel is more with Beulah than with the New Jerusalem), all the
natural scene becomes alive, human, and feminine, and encloses the
poet in an embrace of love:

> Embrace me then, ye Hills, and close me in. . . .
> But I would call thee beautiful, for mild

And soft, and gay, and beautiful thou art,
Dear Valley, having in thy face a smile
Though peaceful, full of gladness.
(lines 110–7)

And when the solitary pair had first entered this valley together in
the winter season, its elements had addressed them as fellow beings:

"What would ye," said the shower,
"Wild Wanderers, whither through my dark domain?"
The sunbeam said, "be happy." When this Vale
We entered, bright and solemn was the sky
That faced us with a passionate welcoming,
And led us to our threshold

—a threshold which in an earlier version of the text had been that
of "a home / Within a home, which was to be" (lines 168–73, and
footnote).

This terminus of all the poet's journeyings is not only home and
paradise, but also a recovered unity and wholeness which he had
experienced nowhere else except "as it found its way into my heart
/ In childhood"; for this "blended holiness of earth and sky" is

A termination, and a last retreat,
A Centre, come from wheresoe'er you will,
A Whole without dependence or defect,
Made for itself; and happy in itself,
Perfect Contentment, Unity entire.
(lines 135–51)

And only here does he find a genuine human community. Man "truly
is alone" only in the "vast Metropolis," where he is "doomed / To
hold a vacant commerce... / With objects wanting life, repelling
love," and where "neighbourhood serves rather to divide / Than to
unite." In this rural place, however, all is on a human scale, a multe-
ity-in-unity in which individuality is preserved in a society which is
a family writ large, and which finds itself thoroughly at home in its
natural milieu.

Society is here
A true Community, a genuine frame
Of many into one incorporate....
One household, under God, for high and low,

> One family, and one mansion . . .
>   possessors undisturbed
> Of this Recess . . . their glorious Dwelling-place.
>   (lines 592–624)

The poet's spiritual home, however, remains ineluctably a paradise of this earth, for in the vale man differs "but little from the Man elsewhere" and exhibits the common qualities of "selfishness, and envy, and revenge . . . / Flattery and double-dealing, strife and wrong" (lines 347–57). But, he asks, is there not a strain of words that shall be "the acknowledged voice of life," and so speak "of solid good / And real evil" in a higher poetic harmony than that of the unalloyed pastoral fantasy—

> More grateful, more harmonious than the breath,
> The idle breath of softest pipe attuned
> To pastoral fancies?
>   (lines 401–9)

For this poetry of real life he dismisses the poetry of wish-fulfillment, "All Arcadian dreams / All golden fancies of the golden Age" engendered by man's "wish to part / With all remembrance of a jarring world" (lines 625–32). Confident of "an internal brightness," he assumes "his office" as a mature artist and announces his manifesto: in this "peaceful Vale . . . / A Voice shall speak, and what will be the Theme?" (lines 660–90, 751–3).

"Home at Grasmere" concludes with the answer to this question, in the passage Wordsworth later excerpted to serve as the Prospectus to the subject and argument of *The Recluse* and all its related poems. This statement in fact epitomizes, and proclaims as valid for other men, what the poet himself has learned from the long and arduous journey of his life that has terminated in Grasmere Vale. The subject, he tells us, will incorporate the narrative of that life itself, in the account of "the transitory Being" who had beheld the "Vision" which constituted his poetic credential, and which it was his unique mission to impart. This vision is of "the Mind of Man," through which he will undertake a poetic journey that must ascend higher than Milton's heaven and sink deeper than Milton's hell. Of this audacious poetic enterprise it will be the high argument that we can re-create the experienced world, and that this new world, despite the inescapable fact of evil and anguish—no less evident in the solitude of "fields and groves" than when they are "barricadoed . . . / Within the walls of cities"—will provide a sufficient paradise to which we have immediate access. Here we return to Wordsworth's central figure whose complex genealogy, widespread currency, and personal significance I undertook, [earlier], to explicate. Only let a man succeed in restoring his lost integrity, by consummating a marital union between his mind and a nature which, to the sensual in their sleep of death, has become a severed and alien reality, and he shall find "Paradise, and groves Elysian . . . A simple produce of the common day."

The Fiction of the Self

Richard J. Onorato

When Wordsworth recalls "one, the fairest of all rivers," he imagines the happiness of infancy and of childhood in one idealized picture of the river, the vale, and the first home. This is the river valley of the Derwent at Cockermouth from which all other vales gain their special affective power for him, even the "beloved vale" of his school years in nearby Hawkeshead, and Grasmere, which later became his "chosen vale." In the "beloved vale" of his school days he learned to live with the fact of his mother's loss and to compensate for his loneliness by finding *in* solitude his intimate and affectionate relationship with Nature. His unconscious feelings, projected into Nature and enacted, as we shall see, in his play, were given expression and found relief. To the extent that the child found contentment in his activities he could seem whole to himself and at home where he felt his heart was, in Nature. In this way, the trauma of separation and the loss of the true heart-and-home feeling of being were expressed in denied form, in activities fixated upon repressed experiences.

The first significant journey undertaken by the child was between these two vales, on the public road over the summit of the hill; and I have derived the emotional significance of the recurrent journey-metaphor from the death that led to the change of vales. Wordsworth simply omits to mention the cause of the change of vales:

From *The Character of the Poet: Wordsworth in* The Prelude. © 1971 by Princeton University Press.

> Fair seed-time had my soul, and I grew up
> Foster'd alike by beauty and by fear;
> Much favor'd in my birthplace, and no less
> In that beloved Vale to which, erelong,
> I was transplanted. Well I call to mind
> ('Twas at an early age, ere I had seen
> Nine summers) when upon the mountain slope
> The frost and breath of frosty wind
>
> (I, 305–12)

In the seed-time of the soul, the soul seems like the self rooted in its natural life. As we shall see, the passage recollecting the first home is the most idealized, simplest, and happiest "recollection" in *The Prelude* [references are to 1805 version unless otherwise noted]; it is more a belief than a memory. But immediately afterwards, we begin to observe the remembered activities of the boy as they became habitual and, I think, indicative of the divided ego. The self is then not merely a transplanted thing, but one unconsciously aware of a lost home, strangely pleased in the activities by which it maintains itself, yet troubled in its pleasures. The metaphorical sense of natural growth as soul-and-tillage gradually changes; it ceases to express Wordsworth's growth and comes instead to characterize an ideal condition to be sought. The growth to poetic self-consciousness becomes a journey for Wordsworth—a journey in the world, through its imagery, and perhaps beneath or beyond it. Becoming the highly self-conscious Poet seems inseparable from attempting to be Wordsworth; and at the same time, having true being implies a return to a prior condition, now idealized as the natural habitat of the contented spirit and of the Poet's spirit.

It seems to me consistent with my interpretation of his unconscious search for the lost object and for the wholeness of being associated with it that Wordsworth imagines the completion of the "journey" as a place to live or as a state of being. Specifically, he imagines either an actual place, metaphorically idealized, like Racedown, where there are the fields of the soul to be worked poetically; or he imagines a state of being which will result when a psychic experience of Imagination-Revelation increases consciousness and makes the soul fertile like the "fertiliz'd Egyptian plain." Then his tillage can bring forth the crop of poetry. It is of great importance, too, that he feels he must achieve this condition, resisting the temptation to lapse into passive and unself-conscious states. As we have observed, the attractiveness of withdrawing into the "one interior life" or the possibility of falling into the "abyss of idealism" both express neurotic fears of being burdened by self-consciousness, and suggest psychosis and death.

When, in Book One, he imagines that "mellower years will bring a *riper* mind," as if time rather than some present activity will bring on the fertile condition for the "crop" of poetry, he feels himself to be weak, to be weakly himself, and to be untrue to himself:

> with no skill to part
> Vague longing that is bred by want of power
> From paramount impulse not to be withstood,
> A timorous capacity from prudence;
> From circumspection, infinite delay.
> Humility and modest awe themselves
> Betray me, serving often for a cloak
> To a more subtle selfishness, that now
> Doth lock my functions up in blank reserve,
> Now dupes me by an over-anxious eye ·
> That with a false activity beats off
> Simplicity and self-presented truth.
>
> (I, 241–51)

The alternative, that of deliberately not trying, of taking refuge in renounced ambition and in the voluptuous condition of inactivity and vacant musing, *then* actually seems preferable to the self-told lies that counsel delay:

> —Ah! better far than this, to stray about
> Voluptuously through fields and rural walks,
> And ask no record of the hours, given up
> To vacant musing, unreprov'd neglect
> Of all things, and deliberate holiday;
> Far better never to have heard the name
> Of zeal and just ambition, than to live
> Thus baffled by a mind that every hour
> Turns recreant to her task, takes heart again,
> Then feels immediately some hollow thought
> Hang like an interdict upon her hopes.
> This is my lot; for either still I find

> Some imperfection in the chosen theme,
> Or see of absolute accomplishment
> Much wanting, so much wanting, in myself,
> That I recoil and droop, and seek repose
> In listlessness from vain perplexity,
> Unprofitably travelling towards the grave,
> Like a false Steward who hath much received
> And renders nothing back.
>
> (I, 252–71)

The questions of what sufficient power is, where it is located, where it comes from, and what inhibits its use are raised by Wordsworth's acute awareness that the pleasurable state of inactivity is a vacant one opposed to the poetic task of being Wordsworth. And it is immediately after his use of the journey–metaphor in conjunction with the prospect of death that the self, which has been set traumatically on its special journey by a death, is given the needed impetus to its task of being the *poetic* self. From the self-asked question: "Was it for this / That one, the fairest of all rivers . . . ," *The Prelude*, in all the peculiarities of its composition and compilation, may be said to follow.

The oblivion of the "one interior life" and the growth of poetic self-consciousness in the Imagination passage are so plainly opposed that the passage on the "one interior life" from MS RV finds no place in *The Prelude*. Both passages propose the union of the self with something greater ("infinitude" or "one mighty whole"), but antithetically in point of self-consciousness. The Imagination passage emphasizes the "I" and the potential of greatness in increased consciousness; the RV passage does the opposite, finding God wherever one cannot distinguish personal characteristics of oneself. Still, the striking inner consistency of Wordsworth's poetic sense of things may be seen by setting the characterizations of these opposite tendencies in him side by side. When he speaks of the "one interior life," he says:

> By such communion I was early taught
> *That what we see of forms and images*
> *Which float along our minds* and what we feel
> Of active, or of recognizable thought,
> Prospectiveness, intelligence or will
> Not only is not worthy to be deemed
> Our being, to be priz'd as what we are,

But is the very littleness of life.
Such consciousnesses seemed by accidents
Relapses from the one interior life
Which is in all things, from that unity
In which all beings live with God, are lost
In God and Nature, in one mighty whole.
(MS RV)

In which all beings live with God, themselves
Are God, existing in one mighty whole.
(MS 2 of "Peter Bell")

On the other hand, when he speaks so very beautifully of seeking
himself in the uncertain imagery of Memory, he sees the same stream
of the mind, its personal forms and images:

As one who hangs down-bending from the side
Of a slow-moving boat, upon the breast
Of a still water, solacing himself
With such discoveries as his eye can make
Beneath him in the bottom of the deep,
Sees many beauteous sights—woods, fishes, flowers,
Grots, pebbles, roots of trees, and fancies more,
Yet often is perplexed and cannot part
The shadow from the substance, rocks and sky,
Mountains and clouds, reflected in the depth
Of the clear flood, from things which there abide
In their true dwelling; now is crossed by gleam
Of his own image, by a sun-beam now,
And wavering motions sent he knows not whence,
Impediments that make his task more sweet;
Such pleasant office have we long pursued
Incumbent o'er the surface of past time
With like success
(IV, 256–73, 1850)

This stream of the mind, the flow of the self in time since birth, is
mentioned by Wordsworth several times and in different ways in
The Prelude. It is likely that the figure of speech is personal rather
than conventional; it, too, is associated with the original vale, the
home near the Derwent with the river outside the nursery window.

This particular epic simile of self-regard reveals the characteristics and the degree of Wordsworth's self-consciousness perfectly: not only is there the usual difficulty of seeing clearly what is in the depths of the stream and of the self in time past, but as one both "solaces" oneself in looking there and "fancies" a certain amount of what one sees, one's own necessary presence adds one's own present motives to the task, distorting it. Having found intuitively a beautiful poetic analogy for his kind of poetic preoccupation, Wordsworth adds the detail that his own present image falls upon the surface of past time, so that he must look into the past by looking into and through himself—which is, in a visual sense, obvious. But at the same time the extended simile reminds us of how the image of his present self comes between him and his past, or rather, how his past tends to give back his own present image of himself while showing at the same time, and however imprecisely, a good deal more of himself beneath it. With a kind of optical inevitability, the simile adds the perceiver and his motives to his perceptions: unparted shadow and substance yield his image of himself as *he* tries to see it, not as someone might see him in his story.

Beyond solace and fancy is the synthesis of the self in time; poetry results from the peculiar tensions of self-consciousness, but as an activity, it moves beyond the acceptance of self-consciousness, hybristically seeking divinity in the consciousness of personal genius. Gradually, Wordsworth reveals the dimensions of the wish he cherishes, and unconsciously he reveals its origins. That Wordsworth joins the human desire to survive to the feeling of continuous and perhaps immortal life felt in poetry (and that he distinguishes both from the selfless "immortal being" of the Christian soul, which moves at death beyond these concerns), the following passage from Book Five makes clear:

> Thou also, Man, hast wrought,
> For commerce of thy nature with itself,
> Things worthy of unconquerable life;
> And yet we feel, we cannot chuse but feel
> That these must perish. Tremblings of the heart
> It gives, to think that the immortal being
> No more shall need such garments; and yet Man,
> As long as he shall be the Child of Earth,
> Might almost 'weep to have' what he may lose,

> Nor be himself extinguish'd; but survive
> Abject, depress'd, forlorn, disconsolate.
>
> (V, 17–27)

Wordsworth implies that in creating or appreciating human things worthy of immortal life man expresses his own desire not to die. But there is also a poetic connection between what Wordsworth says here of man's desire to survive no matter what ("abject, depress'd, forlorn, disconsolate") and the early trauma in his own life that resulted for Wordsworth in such personal poetry. Poetry became the obsessive "commerce" of his nature with itself, revealing his desire to live and his way of being himself. But "depressed" calls to mind the line from the passage about the Blest Babe, which I have suggested characterizes his own unrealized feelings about himself at the time of his mother's death: "No outcast he, bewildered and depress'd." Wordsworth the child had felt outcast, bewildered and depressed (one could add abject, forlorn, disconsolate), yet was "seeking the visible world" in order to survive in it. We have observed some of the ways in which becoming the Poet derives from that attempt to accept the visible world; but we have seen, too, how the mind further induces its psychic and spiritual experiences in a visionary relating of visible to invisible, of outside to inside, of present to absent, and of alive to dead. This is the commerce of Wordsworth's "nature with itself," the commerce of his habitual sense of himself with his spirit's original sense of its wholeness. What Wordsworth thinks poetry is to Man describes what it had gradually become to himself. The feeling of immortality with which poetry teases his mind is accompanied by a displaced acknowledgment of death: Poetry itself may perish. This opening passage of Book Five leads to the remarkable Arab Dream, . . . which opposes the denial and the acceptance of death as they may be imagined or revealed in poetry.

  In its vigor, poetic self-consciousness opposes itself to the imagined union with God in the oblivion of the "one interior life," and seems instead to imagine no limit for itself. It is a temptation to the poetic spirit to find in itself and in its proper activity the very Godliness it seems to risk losing by the assertion of Self. God, Wordsworth says in the passage on the "one interior life," has centrality and wholeness of being within his nature. (One thinks here of Aristotle's self-contemplative God as engaged in the sole activity of the "commerce of his Nature with itself.") But Wordsworth seems consciously to seek his own centrality and Godliness in his poetic account of his growth. If he can fix "the wavering balance" of his mind and show himself how his own story leads to his ideal of himself as the Poet, he will have a Godly understanding of his own being. Poets, ideally described in Book Thirteen, have "the highest bliss that can be known. . . . The consciousness / Of whom they are habitually infused / Through every image, and through every thought." But I have suggested, too, that in a more complex way, he seeks this knowledge unconsciously, unaware of what it entails.

If Wordsworth's sense of his "privileged" growth is to be understood as "traumatic," then the imaginable Godliness of the Poet depends in some way on the survival of the child who suffered in the artist who creates. Wordsworth would not accept the word "suffered," but the poet who said "The child is father of the man" would not have objected to our discerning the crucial presence of the child in the man. Wordsworth wished to make the case that the Poet of Nature, her special child, was comparable only to the God above Nature, as Imagination is to Revelation; and "God," who is not mentioned often, seems to be introduced only for the purpose of this high comparison. Let us first observe, then, that the Poet's autonomy as a creator is to be demonstrated by his powerful and personal use of Nature herself in his creations. Of course, this is not unusual, when one thinks about it; no poet could do less and be a poet. But the claim that Wordsworth makes for the Poet is so striking simply because it occurs to him to give the analogy that peculiar emphasis, exaggerating and insisting upon it. I think that it is to the relevant period of a child's psychology we must turn—the period of infantile omnipotence which culminates in the Oedipus complex.

The "Godliness" of the child is to be seen first according to the family triangle—in the child's desire to assert his autonomy from the mother by asserting his sexual powers in relation to her and his wish to deny the significance of the absent father. Rearranging the principal beings of his world in fantasy, and making the best of what he imagines, he uses his unchecked powers of wishing omnipotently. With them, he demotes the powerful and permissive mother to an object of desire, and at the same time excludes the father whose real power and significance he has begun to observe but has not yet significantly experienced and realized. It is this sense of the permissive mother who allows the self-exalting fantasy to develop that Wordsworth finds in Nature.

In observing what Freud called the fantasies and conflicts of the Oedipal period of growth, we should observe, too, than an eight-year-old child ordinarily has passed through and resolved these conflicts. In the figurative sense of the word, he has already "lost" the mother, and has instead an uncertain and distrustful recollection of her permissiveness which had "betrayed" him to his psychic conflict with the father. I shall attempt to show presently that Wordsworth had undergone that later experience of figuratively "losing" the mother, but that the literal event, the extreme trauma of loss in death, forced upon him the need to deny all loss. The subsequent expressions of regressive need may be understood in terms of this blocking of further normative growth, as may the subsequent unconscious poetic attempt at curing the self. It should hardly need saying that the apparent pathology of the poet affords us a closer look at something more interesting than normative growth and its many reductive adjustments. And that not pathology itself, but the use of the creative mind in a pathological circumstance is what is interesting here. There are many "cases" of unresolvable Oedipal fantasy and conflict, but one cannot even name another great poetic autobiography.

In normative growth, children repress the fantasies and the experiences in which their desire for the mother culminates, as well as repress their former awareness of such desires. Although wishes to possess her continue unconsciously, the figurative sense of the loss of the mother is felt; it is accepted-in-living, but it is not understood. On the one hand, she is still crucially the center of the life of the home, in which the son's growing identification with the father develops; on the other, she is ultimately the cause of his independent search for satisfaction in life. That "independence" is the real degree of autonomy he will achieve in his growth. His restlessness, his unconscious feelings of desire, of danger, of betrayal, and of loss, lead him specifically away from her as an object of desire after puberty, and yet towards something suggestive of her and of the original love relationship with her. Every finding in reality is a refinding, Freud observed (in *On Narcissism*). What persisted for Wordsworth, however, because of the greater need to deny the experience of her absolute loss is the fantasy of unimpaired possession of the mother "within" him, and, in her projected form, around him as the Presence in Nature. His special sense of the power of a Poet derives from the enormous powers of fantasy originally associated with her permissiveness, now felt by projection as Nature's permissiveness.

Both the habit of action and the limits of imaginable action that sons acquire are normatively modeled on the father as they identify themselves with him after their initial conflict with him. But the need to deny the irreparable loss of the mother, as Wordsworth experienced it, prevented further identification with the father and caused regression from it; so, too, did his actual separation from his father in the ensuing years in which the schoolboy saw his absent father only at holidays. Hence, both the habit of action and the limits of imaginable action reverted to those of an earlier period. This is to say that the fixated mind occupies itself with recreating the world it inhabits rather than with adjusting to the one that is there. Fixation is like an arrest of growth in the period in which play-fantasy dominates a child's being, limiting the extent and the kinds of action undertaken in reality. For the duration of childhood there is a latency period in which what is repressed may be comparatively quiescent, in so far as present reality does not make demands on the ego too great for it to answer while it attempts to maintain itself in this way. Many of the most ordinary habits of action, assertion, and competition are left undeveloped where fantasy predominates; for the ego can maintain itself even in solitude, and often more successfully so, without the impositions made on it by other people's needs and actions. But there is, too, the tendency in the self-aggrandizing and assertive fantasies of the pre-Oedipal and Oedipal periods to bring on the conflict with the father who seems to be sought out in order to be denied his significance. We shall see presently how this is applicable to Wordsworth's discovery of himself as "the favored being" of Nature. It is as if, beyond fantasy, his imagination were unconsciously seeking conflict.

Writing poetry, for instance, while not competitive and assertive in the usual sense of assertion among men, had for Wordsworth that same quality of fantastic and incestuous assertion present in the period of infantile fantasy I have been describing. The Poet's desire to name poetry as man's highest activity and to make the Poet's mind comparable to God's mind makes in fact the same connection between the Poet and God in point of Nature that the child once made between the child and the father in point of the mother. The Poet, Wordsworth says, fostered by Nature, can then use her as he wishes, creating out of her elements things of his own, as a God would. But when a child's fantasies initiate his Oedipal conflicts, it is because, among other things, he has already begun to perceive the finer autonomy of the absent father. The father is the man who comes and goes, who is and is not there, but whose power is believed by others. The child has begun to compare that autonomous power with his own powers as he has exercised them in his own willful pursuits. In wanting to render his father insignificant, he is only denying a model of power he has begun to admire and envy, and one that he has begun to perceive more or less accurately in relation to the mother and to himself. The ensuing experience of conflict with the father permanently fixes the normative sense of self and the subsequent degree of autonomy for a boy. One should observe that this, too, is a kind of fixation, a "normative" one.

When Wordsworth writes, in Book Five, of growth as a diminution of powers, he gives a perfect characterization of poetry as the omnipotence of wishing opposed to the common acceptances of life. The Poet persists in using his powers of creation, imitating the God of creation:

> Dumb yearnings, hidden appetites are ours,
> And they must have their food: our childhood sits,
> Our simple childhood sits upon a throne
> That hath more power than all the elements.
> I guess not what this tells of Being past,
> Nor what it augurs of the life to come;
> But so it is; and in that dubious hour,
> That twilight when we first begin to see
> This dawning earth, to recognise, expect;
> And in the long probation that ensues,
> The time of trial, ere we learn to live
> In reconcilement with our stinted powers,
> To endure this state of meagre vassalage;
> Unwilling to forego, confess, submit,
> Uneasy and unsettled; yoke-fellows
> To custom, mettlesome, and not yet tam'd
> And humbled down, oh! then we feel, we feel,
> We know when we have Friends. Ye dreamers, then,
> Forgers of lawless tales! we bless you then,
> Imposters, drivellers, dotards, as the ape
> Philosophy will call you: then we feel
> With what, and how great might ye are in league,
> Who make our wish our power, our thought a deed,

> An empire, a possession; Ye whom Time
> And Seasons serve; all Faculties; to whom
> Earth crouches, th' elements are potter's clay,
> Space like a Heaven fill'd up with Northern lights;
> Here, nowhere, there, and everywhere at once.
>
> (V, 530–57)

Invoking "the poets"—those of his and of everyone's impressionable years—Wordsworth simulates the wonder and implies the wisdom of the child. Philosophers and common men no longer know that once their wishes were powers, their thoughts deeds. Ultimately, poets gain only other poets as followers—seekers of truer homes, of deeper and prior realities, of invisible worlds, of fertile fields of the spirit, of lost empires and lost possessions. But in *The Prelude* Wordsworth is attempting to assure himself of his own possession of this very power; and, having considered the impoverishment of the human mind by man's loss of it, he intends in his future poetry to assault the dull minds of men, to remind them of their own lost feelings and powers. The Poet in his role is rather self-assertively some sort of God handling "the elements." Moralizing and beautifying the commonplace, like Jesus, he tells man to be instructed by regarding the lesser celandines and the daffodils of the field and by hearing the Apocalyptic blasts of the waterfall.

To many hungry in spirit, the Poet is Godly generous. But the Poet is also a spirit who tells man that there is no acceptable limit for knowledge, that he is to acquire again the Godly powers of mind that once were his and that should be his, as perhaps Satan would. If Jesus is the Divine Child of the Mother who must first free himself from her to go about his father's business, Satan, in Milton's version of him, would understand himself to be, like Imagination to Wordsworth, "unfathered." But Wordsworth, of course, is not attending to these implications of the Poet's powers; he accepts only limited liability for his personal fiction. The Jesus who really "replaces" the father he perfectly serves and the Satan who cannot depose the father he will not serve are the two aspects of the ambivalent relationship of the Son with the Father as Western man has imagined the conflicts of his personal will to power. The Son is at one with the Father or at war with him. As Freud observed, Man seems unable to free himself of his unconscious ambivalence for the primary beings of his dependent childhood.

But we should observe, too, that the feelings of dread felt at the beginning of *The Prelude* by the Poet—the "deadening admonitions," the hollow thoughts that "hang like an interdict" upon his hopes—must derive from this same circumstance of incipient conflict with the father. As Wordsworth intended to announce the Godly self-sufficiency of the Poet, he was unconsciously approaching the subject of freedom from the mother. He was also unconsciously approaching the repressed experience of Oedipal conflict with the father, an experience ever more deeply "repressed" than the specific trauma and fixation from which he was seeking unconsciously to free himself. It is no accident, then, that in Book One, speaking of his inability to proceed with the poem, he speaks of

> Vague longing that is bred by want of power
> From paramount impulse not to be withstood,
> A timorous capacity from prudence;
> From circumspection, infinite delay.
>
> (I, 241–4)

He is echoing the devil's synod in Book Two of *Paradise Lost*—the devils sullenly considering their own powers in rivalry with God's.

In his experience of fixated growth Wordsworth was not free to identify himself strongly with the father, whose own early death when Wordsworth was thirteen made the difficult psychic circumstance of the boy even more precarious. Circumstantially excluded from many of the normal experiences of identification from boyhood to manhood, Wordsworth discovered, adapted, and invented the role of Poet, his personal fiction. But one can see in his story his inability to learn simply the ways of men and to undergo their rituals of initiation. He could not imitate and accept. He habitually renounced action and competition, both at school and in the choice of career. His father had been a lawyer, but Wordsworth, in writing about his period of crisis (in Books Ten and Eleven) uses law, law-courts, and lawyers as a key metaphor for conveying his desperation: he felt unable to "defend" his own convictions, his feelings about the natural rightness of the Revolutionary cause. How, then, are we to see the psychological situation of the Poet in relation to what we might call the normative-historical experience of growth?

Freud derived the fear of death and the fear of individuality from the fear of separation from the mother and from castration anxiety. When the mother becomes an object of premature genital desire, the father is feared as a castrating figure; and the child's wish to do away with his father is perceived fearfully by the child, in its projected form, as the father's desire to kill the child. This psychic ordeal, which results in the fearful renunciation of the mother, the repression of unacceptable wishes, and the subsequent identification of the child with the father, is at the same time an historical ordeal, which fathers too have suffered in their growth. In this way, the structures and processes of historical societies come to reflect the personalities of men, since communities maintain institutionally the repressions by which men live. Repressed infantile wishes in men can neither gain the expression they continue to seek, nor be *seen* clearly so that possibly they could be relinquished when understood. Thus, repressed infantile conflicts permanently confuse man's feelings about desire, castration, and death, besetting him with unconscious fears that preclude true individuality. Between separation from the mother and ritual initiation into the community, there has always been the abnormality of neurotic self-consciousness, for which the human temperament has ever sought palliatives and employments; but when we discuss the abnormal "infantile" origins of the life-style of the Poet, we must bear in mind the implicit comparison with the normal "infantile" origins of the life-style of historical societies.

The Poet, to the extent that Wordsworth exemplifies him, is unconsciously compelled to return to infantile trauma. Unable to ignore the disturbance he continues to feel about loss and growth in his own past, he unconsciously expresses the doubts he feels compelled to deny; and still he achieves no lasting composure. Therefore, he undertakes to examine his growth more elaborately, with an imaginative theory about his growth that is a personal fiction. Consequently, he must express profound dissatisfaction with normative growth, and he indicts society and History. For if his growth is, as he believes, natural, then that of historical societies is unnatural. His sympathy with the French Revolution seems entirely natural to him; he was led to the Revolution by Nature.

In writing Books Eight to Ten of *The Prelude*, especially the parts dealing directly with France, the French Revolution and his crisis, Wordsworth was unsure of what to say his actions in that period meant. He could not say of himself what I think can be said about him in that period, that he was unconsciously seeking the ordeal that might free him from the fixated condition of his psyche, which had by then become such a burden to his young manhood.

In idealizing the principles of the Revolution as they would be asserted against and tested by an historical reality and by men who were basically so different from the Poet, he was asserting himself as a "natural being in the strength of Nature." But unconsciously he knew about the undependability of the source of such strength. Were he to see that his natural sympathies with the Revolution were Nature's way of "betraying" him to the experience of what men in History are "really" like, he might bring upon himself the repressed traumatic feelings of the past. He would have to make himself understand why Nature had seemed to set him apart from men so early in life. And were he subsequently to see himself in this way in his poetry, he would see the young Poet standing alone in the middle of his ordeal, as in fact he did stand alone, though he did not see it clearly.

The Eye and Progress of His Song: A Lacanian Reading of *The Prelude*

Robert Young

> The other *darkness is that of the elusive psyche, or the supposed*
> *subject of psychoanalytic investigation. The closer we get to that subject*
> *the less of a subject it is: the ego, personal center,* sujet *or signified,*
> *dissolves into a field of forces and is depicted by unstable diagrams,*
> *"with cycles and epicycles scribbled o'er."*
> Geoffrey Hartman

Tremendous blunders:
1. the absurd overestimation of consciousness, the transformation
of it into a unity, an entity: 'spirit', 'soul', something that feels,
thinks, wills—
2. spirit as cause, especially wherever purposiveness, system, co-
ordination appear;
3. consciousness as the highest achievable form, as the supreme kind
of being, as 'God';

It could have been a critique of Wordsworth. Few nineteenth-century
writers were as prepared as Nietzsche to acknowledge the necessity
of incompleteness and fragmentariness or the fiction of the spirit;
instead they favoured what was to be the Hegelian aspiration and
description of consciousness ("unhappy consciousness," the "beautiful soul," etc.):

From *The Oxford Literary Review* 3, no. 3 (Spring 1979). © 1979 by *The Oxford
Literary Review*.

> an organised structure of self-apprehension which entails
> and includes a plurality of moments, an entire coherent
> discourse that is never actualized in its totality (a "con-
> sciousness," a "*Bewusstsein*").

A work can become a "totality" by the very fact of completion, but
the claim of "organic form" for it may only reveal its motivating
"intense desire." And that desire may itself emerge as a desire for a
totality, a unity of the subject of consciousness, the ability to construct an unfragmented discourse, Voice. The claim for *The Prelude*
is often that it is organised along "more associational than logical"
lines. But the inner logic is there: the logic of repetition, desire, the
quest for the *objet a*.

This reading of *The Prelude* will be antithetical in that it will
read the poem by an inversion/subversion of Wordsworth's own
terms. Lacan's work precludes the possibility of its being read as a
presentation of authentic, epiphanic experience; it redeprives His
Majesty the Ego (whether of poet or critic) of his pretensions to a
unified consciousness; while it no longer allows us to see sublimation
as the displacement of desire into art, but rather as the very structure
of desire itself, passing into phantoms "Of texture midway betwixt
life and books" (III, 613). [References to *The Prelude* are to the 1805
version unless otherwise noted.] Instead, as Jeffrey Mehlman has
argued, art becomes an exemplary fiction which "the (imaginary)
self tells itself in order to defend its (illusory) sense of autonomy,"
and structure becomes "a self-regulating series of transformations of
a constant system of relationships." Wordsworth's own fiction (which
he calls truth) is the concept of the imagination. At the end of *The
Prelude*, he declaims authoritatively:

> This faculty hath been the moving soul
> Of our long labour: we have traced the stream
> From darkness, and the very place of birth
> In its blind cavern, whence is faintly heard
> The sound of waters
>
> (XIII, 171–5)

From the sound by the Derwent to the final "feeling of life endless,
the great thought / By which we live, Infinity and God" (XIII, 183–
4), it has been the "soul," the power of the poem. But insofar as it
has been found, it has also been the object of quest, a quest which,

as Lacan suggests, necessarily finds the subject "inserted in a function whose exercise grasps it"—which is to say that Wordsworth, in pursuing imagination, is in fact caught within the function that occurs in its locus. In the same way, implications about the relation of the imagination to the "under soul" (III, 540) will be read by the antithetical light of the Freudian discovery. For the Freudian unconscious

> is not all the romantic unconscious of imaginative creation.
> . . . To all . . . forms of unconscious, ever more or less linked to some obscure will regarded as primordial, to something preconscious, what Freud opposes is the revelation that at the level of the unconscious there is something at all points homologous with what occurs at the level of the subject—this thing speaks and functions in a way quite as elaborate as at the level of the conscious, which thus loses what seemed to be its privilege.

The unconscious, as Lacan defines it, is "lacuna, cut, rupture inscribed in a certain lack."

Following and reinterpreting Freud, Lacan's project has been to recentre the subject "as speaking in the very lacunae of that in which, at first sight, it presents itself as speaking." Such a project invites comparison with the division in the subject that is articulated by Geoffrey Hartman in his essay "Romanticism and Anti-Self-Consciousness." The difficulty for Romantic poets that Hartman describes is that whereas each poet seeks a return to a "Unity of Being," every increase in consciousness is accompanied by an increase in self-consciousness. The antidote to this is drawn from consciousness itself:

> The principle of restoration is found in thought, and thought only: the hand that inflicts the wound is also the hand that heals it.

The desire to overcome self-consciousness is a part of the dialectical movement of the mind and of poetry itself—which presents even consciousness as a "kind of death-in-life, as the product of a division in the self."

> In "Tintern Abbey," or 'X' Revisited, the poet looks back at a transcended stage and comes to grips with the fact of self-alienation . . . For the Romantic 'I' emerges nostalgically when certainty and simplicity of self are lost.

What remains is the dialectic between "the relatively self-conscious self and that self within the self. The problem of subjectivity and solipsism becomes the subject of poems even as they seek to transmute it:

> This paradox seems to inhere in all the seminal works of the Romantic period. "Thus my days are passed / In contradiction," Wordsworth writes sadly at the beginning of *The Prelude*. He cannot decide whether he is fit to be a poet on an epic scale. The great longing is there; the great (objective) theme eludes him. Wordsworth cannot find his theme because he knows he already has it: himself. Yet he knows self-consciousness to be at once necessary and opposed to poetry.

The myth of the Fall is seen as a defense against the self-conscious intellect: consciousness and self-consciousness become knowledge and guilt. The burden of self is opposed to that which might dissolve it and reestablish innocence: in Wordsworth's case "the wound of self" is healed by "unconscious intercourse" with nature. "The art of the Romantics . . . is often in advance of even their best thoughts"; this article may be conceived of as developing or retheorising the impossible dialectic that Hartman finds.

Wordsworth compares the structure of *The Prelude* with that of the Fall in *Paradise Lost*, but there is no discernible actual fall, like Satan's into the opened wound of Chaos. Instead it is constituted by his failure to produce the harmony and voice of a God: "God-like power" (IV, 156), a totality that can rival the idealised imago of the precursor's Magian power and control. Beset by failure, impediments, the subject is fractured—"he feels lost, stopped, halted, split into separate beings." And in the impediment, failure, fracture, Lacan finds the unconscious, its discontinuity and vacillation: "The unconscious is always manifested as that which vacillates in a split in the subject, from which emerges a discovery that Freud compares with desire . . . ." Against the narcissistic identifications with an idealised self, the subject finds himself a fading coal in the shadowy ground between the unconscious and the conscious, between being and meaning. And in the absent space of the fracture, the site of lack, rises up the evanescent mist or phantom of the imagination, which we may reinterpret as desire, the *objet a*, the "something evermore about to be" (VI, 542). The strategy for the stabilising, the binding, of the fractured self is the "immobilization of desire," but this always eludes the subject (necessarily) and he remains in a state of vacillation. The "imperishable restlessness" of desire that is always elsewhere is assuaged by the return to memory, which Wordsworth names the hiding-place of his power (XI, 336). Against this idealistic view of memory, the antithetical critic must set the insistence of Freud that the "experience of memory has less to do with the recollection of an event than with the repetition of a structure":

> Recollection is not Platonic reminiscence—it is not the return of a form, an imprint, a *eidos* of beauty and good, a supreme truth, coming to us from the beyond. It is something that comes to us from the structural necessities, something humble, born at the level of the lowest encounters.

In memory, Lacan detects the structure of the encounter, the essential encounter "to which we are always called with a real that eludes us." And insofar as the encounter is "essentially the missed encounter" the elusion/illusion is perpetrated in an endless repetition of desire. This repetition-compulsion is grounded in "the very split that occurs in the subject in relation to the encounter," and so bears the death-drive "in its function as matrix of desire and as essential support of the castration complex": the "central peace, subsisting at the heart / Of endless agitation."

"Perhaps his mind dislikes a vacuum and strives to convert absence into presence" suggests Hartman. In the vacant place in the split, "the lack of a lack," emerges the *objet a*. Prey to the duplicity that will never allow a return to the originating impulse, but instead always perpetrate the circuits of desire, Wordsworth is led to locate the *objet a* in nature—water, mist, wind, objects that heal fractures, that fill gaps. *The Prelude's* ideal is to retrieve the imagination/*objet a* from objects outside the self to something within—when paradoxically in a Berkeleyan splendour they have never appeared anywhere else. The imagination, the phallic ghost, must rise within him to raise him to the height, power, voice of the Miltonic challenge:

> for who, though with the tongue
> Of angels, can relate, or to what things
> Liken on earth conspicuous, that may lift

> Human imagination to such highth
> Of Godlike power
> (*Paradise Lost* VI, 297–301)

No one can. For Wordsworth there will only be "the sadness of incompletion," a perpetual process of fading as he stands, "lost within himself / In trepidation" (VI, 425), at "the blank abyss," in the space of vacancy, "constantly occupied, it seems, in mastering the primordial unconscious without ever really succeeding—or if so, at what a price . . ."

II

It is unlikely that the interpreter can come to a firm conclusion on the nature of the felt absence.

The Prelude was written because Wordsworth was unable to write *The Recluse*, the philosophical epic that was to usurp the place of *Paradise Lost*. It was above all poetic power for which he was questing: priority, a stance of his own, voice. It is voice that is specified at the beginning of the poem as lacking:

> my soul
> Did once again make trial of the strength
> Restored to her afresh; nor did she want
> Eolian visitations; but the harp
> Was soon defrauded, and the banded host
> Of harmony dispersed in straggling sounds
> And, lastly, utter silence.
>
> (I, 101–7)

Just so waked Satan: against this loss of "harmony divine" the poet places the voice of nature, very often the sound of running water. Michael Riffaterre has drawn attention to what he calls "the *sound of waters* structure" in Wordsworth's poetry, where the sound becomes "symbolic of a power stronger than death." In the sound vs. man's fear of death opposition, the "overwhelming superiority of A over B is transformed into the equivalence of B and A, or even reversed, since B, the sound, annuls A, Man's fear." For Bloom, death for a poet is less a literal than a poetic death, a death which is his own but which he survives. But this Satanic eclipse can also be seen as the moment of alienation, castration, separation, in the development of the subject when it undergoes the *Spaltung*, the split that occurs at the moment of the appearance of the subject in the signifying chain, which is also the moment of the differentiation of the unconscious and the conscious:

> the subject appears first in the Other, insofar as the first signifier, the unary signifier, emerges in the field of the Other and represents the subject for another signifier, which other signifier has as its effect the *aphanisis* of the subject. Hence the division of the subject—when the subject appears somewhere as meaning, he is manifested elsewhere as 'fading', as disappearance. There is, then, one might say, a matter of life and death between the unary signifier and the subject, *qua* binary signifier, cause of his disappearance.

The constant appearance and disappearance of the subject in language is described as the process of alienation, the effect of which is the division of the subject who appears only in that division. The moment of fracture and articulation is the moment of castration which initiates the perpetual process of displacement, the ludic sliding of desire that forever seeks to fill the lack by which the subject is constituted. Repositing, then, the opposition *water murmuring / dulls the pangs of mortality* in these terms, it is the breach in the subject himself that the sound of the waters seems to fill, offering a resolution of the dialectic of "the impossible coincidence of the 'I', the subject of the enunciation, with the 'I', the subject of the utterance." In Wordsworth's myth, the sound of running waters gives a wholeness like that of the infant, where no fracture has come to alienate being and meaning. Hence the assuaging identification of the river with his own mind; the one is set up as the guarantor of the other, set indissolubly together:

> Was it for this
> That one, the fairest of all Rivers, loved
> To blend his murmurs with my Nurse's song,
> And from his alder shades and rocky falls,
> And from his fords and shallows, sent a voice
> That flowed along my dreams? For this, didst Thou,
> O Derwent! travelling over the green Plains
> Near my 'sweet birthplace', didst thou, beauteous Stream,
> Make ceaseless music through the night and day
>
> (I, 271–9)

The 'voice' of the river's murmurings and Wordsworth's own poetic voice coalesce only in a play of desire. It is the play of the child that holds them apart. In Freud's *fort / da* example, while the child seeks to master its mother's absence by the repeated cry of there! gone! the cotton-reel that it throws masks the partial satisfaction of its mastery:

> For the game of the cotton-reel is the subject's answer to what the mother's absence has created on the frontier of his domain—the edge of his cradle—namely, a *ditch*, around which one can only play at jumping.

Against the cry of the child is what "is not there, *qua* represented"; the cotton-reel "takes the place of the representation" as *objet a* in the gap of self-mutilation, of lack and desire.

> The *objet a* is something from which the subject, in order to constitute itself, has separated itself off as organ. This serves as a symbol of the lack, that is to say, of the phallus, not as such, but insofar as it is lacking.

"This object, which is in fact simply the presence of a hollow, a void" emerges from the primal splitting of the subject. The murmuring sound, absent yet present, which Wordsworth identifies as the key that will unlock his "functions" from their "blank reserve" (I, 248) and towards which he is driven, is the elusive symbol that can fill the crack of separation, the "other reality hidden behind the lack of that which takes the place of representation." The subject resists its loss, but its irreparable absence causes the continual flight from one signifier to another. Water, mist, wind, the lure of the gaze in the landscape: *The Prelude* maps an inevitable perpetration that can never stop up "the lack inscribed in the subject from the start by the very fact of his being eclipsed as a signifier." "Every object of desire, every object of alienating identification will reveal itself to be necessarily ephemeral and destined to be supplanted": the poem winds its way from one moment of assuagement of lack to another, questing in a quest that can never be realised; the circumspection and infinite delay of the divided subject are infinite. A voice such as that of nature can never heal the split of alienation—it remains a ghostly wish, a presentiment of a perpetual and tantalising possibility.

In that realm [of the imagination] things are not what or where they are. They dwell in a continual flickering displacement, the displacement described in the splendid metaphor of the aurora borealis in Book Five of *The Prelude* to define the strange space of those verbal fictions "forged" by the imagination: "Space like a heaven filled up with northern lights, / Here, nowhere, there, and everywhere at once."

As against the infinite variety of displacements that mask self-mutilation, "what analytic experience enables us to declare is rather the limited function of desire." The subject remains suspended on the thread of the cotton-reel, in a state of radical vacillation:

> I deem not profitless those fleeting moods
> Of shadowy exultation: not for this,
> That they are kindred to our purer mind
> And intellectual life; but that the soul,
> Remembering how she felt, but what she felt
> Remembering not, retains an obscure sense
> Of possible sublimity, to which
> With growing faculties she doth aspire,
> With faculties still growing, feeling still
> That whatsoever point they gain, they still
> Have something to pursue.
>
> (II, 331–41)

In Spring 1798, when this was written, Wordsworth was looking out to the beyond; *The Prelude* reveals the uncanny fact that the beyond is also behind, on the other side, behind the veil of representation.

If nature is able to tantalise with an originating and undivided voice ("nor word from word could I divide,"), then so is the precursor—"the deity of prescience"—and his priority of a totalising strength as he is idealised in the mind of the ephebe. The reaction of the belated poet is a process of accommodation to his own fracture by resort to the screen—for a poet, language:

> he isolates the function of the screen and plays with it. Man, in effect, knows how to play with the mask as that beyond which there is the gaze. The screen is here the locus of mediation.

The mimicry of a poet or a Winander Boy is "distinct from what might be called an *itself* that is behind." To mask his non-appearance in the realm of the signifier as subject, the poet deploys travesty, intimidation, imitation. The true subject of *The Prelude* behind its veil of representation is the indeterminacy of its subject, the absence of undifferentiated voice, the "spacious gap" and confounded roar of the abyss of Chaos. The eclipse of being at the moment of meaning invalidates any claim for a priority that can rival the voice of the precursor. Instead, the poem seeks to make its stance and to stake its claims by stealth, to generate a 'lost' unity by a travesty that dissolves its own fracture. The poem masks itself and its gaps by a gradual accretion of moments—"this *belong to me* aspect of representations. so reminiscent of property"—that play with the evanescence of the *objet a*, a broken trajectory of narcissistic idealisations of a (mythical) past self that can be given a locus and enclosed stature in the memory-text or text-as-memory rivalling the presence of the precursor. "But what sovereign subject is the origin of the book?"

The awareness displayed of the fading of the subject radically undermines the (lost) possibility of the *cogito*: the speaker does not speak for a determinate being. Instead he is minimally aware that it is in the locus of the unconscious that being resides—and that this being is essentially unassimilable with the subject of consciousness. This being from which the subject of consciousness is split is idealised as the self of childhood, and it is there that truth is situated. Since this truth has been lost, the function of the poem and of the imagination is one of represencing. "If what Wordsworth represents in his poetry is an absence, does not the term 'representation' become questionable?" Imagination, the represencer of a lost totality and healer of wounds, is the fantasmatic goal of Wordsworth's quest, haunting him with its lure of an I-magus power of the mind over itself and its own evanescence. It becomes the idealised imago that presents itself in the face of the mind's own division, image of the esemplastic faculty and undivided power. As imago, artificial representation of an object, the 'waxen image' which he himself has made, it is a suitable term for the desired stability of the *objet a*. But can't the imago as representation also be the imago as phantom, ghost or apparition? Stability is undermined even by the images of the imagination themselves: wind and mist—"that is . . . two atmospheric phenomena which are mutually exclusive." If representation is a represencing, still it provides no master such as Freud supposed, nor even that of "emotion recollected in tranquillity." The real will always prove to be elusive, the encounter is the *dustuchia*, the "encounter forever missed," and will never be resolved to a last instance.

The Spots of Time:
Spaces for Refiguring

David E. Simpson

If space is the theatre of figurative representation, then time is the measure of its continuance or disappearance, and the oxymoron at the heart of Wordsworth's famous phrase gives us a clue to the nature and resolution of such representations. Because the spots are of *time*, they are not to be held within any stable perspective, not to be visualized or fixed by the look. They are identities whose very definition supposes *process*, monuments of creative instability.

One of the most frequently reiterated aspects of the poet's youth and early maturity in *The Prelude* is its antithetical or oxymoronic experience of nature. "Foster'd alike by beauty and by fear" (I, 306), there is from the first a sense that what nature teaches the child is not any simple harmony with the world, but a continually evolving oscillation between extremes of identity and difference, synthesis and opposition. [References are to the 1805 version unless otherwise noted.] These "Severer interventions" (I, 370) produce a personality based on the capacity to hold together through time experiences of radically different kinds. Here "fear and love" (XIII, 143) will be equally at home,

> With the adverse principles of pain and joy,
> Evil as one is rashly named by those
> Who know not what they say.
> $\qquad$ (XIII, 147–9)

From *Wordsworth and the Figurings of the Real*. © 1982 by David E. Simpson. Macmillan and Humanities Press, Inc., 1982.

The "soothing influences of nature" are thus derived not only from rebirth but also from passing away, from the "types of renovation and decay." Only in this way can pleasure itself be prevented from solidifying into fixed form, subservient to

> The tendency, too potent in itself,
> Of habit to enslave the mind. I mean
> Oppress it by the laws of vulgar sense,
> And substitute a universe of death,
> The falsest of all worlds, in place of that
> Which is divine and true.
>
> (XIII, 138–43)

The insistence on the assimilation of the different aspects of nature through time also involves the mind's active response to what it is given; the mind must 'figure' the materials which are to hand into redisposed forms, providing whatever degree of activity or passivity nature seems not to provide. This is exactly how Wordsworth describes the imagination, a faculty inescapably figurative in that it does not seek to reflect but to refract or reconstruct what is before it. In the preface to *Poems, 1815*, Wordsworth thus describes the imagination as it operates on "images independent of each other":

> These processes of imagination are carried on either by conferring additional properties upon an object, or abstracting from it some of those which it actually possesses, and thus enabling it to re-act upon the mind which hath performed the process, like a new existence.

He then specifies a second activity of the imagination, that "upon images in conjunction by which they modify each other," wherein

> the conferring, the abstracting, and the modifying powers of the Imagination, immediately and mediately acting, are all brought into conjunction.

Clearly, these two operations correspond to two types of figure. The former, working on images in isolation, involves the metonym or synecdoche; hence Wordsworth's example of the cuckoo being represented by means of its song, in a way which "dispossesses the creature almost of a corporeal existence." The second activity of the imagination, working on images in conjunction, is exemplified by the famous example of the stanza from "Resolution and Independence," the one beginning "As a huge stone is sometimes seen to lie." Here the three images, the stone, the sea-beast and the old man, are indeed brought into conjunction, but by a process which involves ignoring some of the qualities of each in order to stress those which are held in common:

> The stone is endowed with something of the power of life to approximate it to the sea-beast; and the sea-beast stripped of some of its vital qualities to assimilate it to the stone; which intermediate image is thus treated for the purpose of bringing the original image, that of the stone, to a nearer resemblance to the figure and condition of the aged Man; who is divested of so much of the indications of life and motion as to bring him to the point where the two objects unite and coalesce in just comparison.

The clarity in Wordsworth's discourse, as it intimates the negative implications in what it is celebrating, is astonishing. The imagination has "no reference to images that are merely a faithful copy," and the "operations of the mind" which it thus involves invoke the mind's highest faculty. But the price of that exalted status may be very high if it is not scrupulously restrained. In both the above detailed kinds of imaginative activity, the metonymic and the metaphoric, Wordsworth makes it clear that there is a 'taking away' of vital qualities. The cuckoo almost loses "corporeal existence" (and there is no easy metaphysic of a transcendent spiritual identity put in its place), and the old man loses the signs of life and motion. If the rhetorical effect of poetry be to insinuate a particular 'way of seeing,' then there are obvious risks in encouraging this kind of selectivity among the imaginative; that is why the doings of Wordsworth's speakers are so often implicitly or explicitly qualified, and why the after effect of the figurative experience is often an education *into* generosity.

Thus the "consolidating numbers into unity, and dissolving and separating unity into number" which constitutes the highest pleasure of imagination, inescapably invokes the possibility of the freak of power. Given that this activity is also necessary and healthful, we can see the importance of that discipline in nature which 'fights back' and refuses to allow such moments of control to endure through *time*. This cycle of experience, involving the correction of the interpretations held at one moment by the perceptions of another, is exactly what we find exemplified in the passages illustrating the "spots of time."

The threat is intimated from the start as the poet defines such moments as those wherein we have the "deepest feeling" that the mind

> Is lord and master, and that outward sense
> Is but the obedient servant of her will.
>
> (XI, 272–3)

This lordship and mastery, which would seem to admit all the negative functions of the figurative imagination, is however qualified by the examples which follow. There are two of them, the experience of the pond and gibbet (XI, 279 ff.) and that of the father's death (XI, 346 ff.).

The first of these passages describes the poet coming upon the gibbet in early childhood, and the sense of "visionary dreariness" (XI, 311) which invested the whole landscape as a consequence of this sighting. Later in life, the adult poet comes to live in "daily presence of this very scene" (XI, 320); familiarity and the society of those he loves now render it acceptable and even a place of joy, informed by "The spirit of pleasure and youth's golden gleam" (XI, 323). What is most significant here is the suggestion that the later experiences are *more* pleasurable *because* of the force of those earlier, antithetical memories. The mind endows the landscape with excess value precisely because it had formerly seemed (or been made to seem) so threatening. Through time, therefore, two extremes of negative and positive evaluation combine to produce a kind of balance. The pain of one perception is answered by subsequent pleasure, and the pleasure itself is tempered by the memory of pain. The figuring mind has, implicitly, been made wary of wholehearted investment in the figurings of any one moment. It has been made to, or has made itself understand that mastery must be seen together with slavery as two extremes of an ongoing and mediating process.

In the second example, the poet describes how, as a schoolboy, he had been so anxious for the holidays to begin, that he climbed to the top of a crag to try to spy out the approach of the horses which were to carry him home. Then we are told, simply, that his father died ten days after he did arrive home,

> And I and my two Brothers, Orphans then,
> Followed his body to the Grave. The event

> With all the sorrow which it brought appear'd
> A chastisement; and when I call'd to mind
> That day so lately pass'd, when from the crag
> I look'd in such anxiety of hope,
> With trite reflections of morality,
> Yet in the deepest passion, I bow'd low
> To God, who thus corrected my desires.
>
> (XI, 367–75)

The juxtaposition of these events is not explained, but we may infer that the death of the father, happening as it does at an irrevocable moment in time, stands in the poet's mind as an answer to that earlier desire to speed up the passing of time. The wish for the earlier arrival of the horses then comes to seem as if it involved also a wish that the moment of the bereavement should come sooner. It is as if the prior dissatisfaction with what had been given is punished by having something taken away. It is a strange, though not at all unconvincing gesture which has the child read himself into a position of responsibility for the father's death, and the subsequently informed adult voice of the narrative may mean to signal as much in making reference to the "trite reflections of morality" which were part of the "deepest passion"; as if the course of events in the world could really be that coherent! The syntax expressing this conjunction of triteness and passion, moreover, allows it to be referred both to the moment of chastisement and to the initial "anxiety of hope." This is appropriate, for the two moments are not different in kind—they both belong to the ongoing figuring of experience outside which Wordsworth offers himself no authoritative position.

This particular antithesis, which may be seen to involve a reminder of the objectivity of time after a wishful attempt to speed it up, is itself assimilated in later life. The images and events which are associated with the top of the crag come to seem

> spectacles and sound to which
> I often would repair and thence would drink,
> As at a fountain; and I do not doubt
> That in this later time, when storm and rain
> Beat on my roof at midnight, or by day
> When I am in the woods, unknown to me
> The workings of my spirit thence are brought.
>
> (XI, 383–9)

The whole cycle of 'transgression' and punishment now becomes restorative, and continually restorative, as the fountain both quenches the thirst of the moment and yet continues to flow. The confidence which accrues from this seems to consist in the insight that the mind can contain and survive such antithetical events, and put them to the service of a continually evolving identity.

Both examples of the operations of "spots of time" then seem to involve a recognition and acceptance of the notion that the figurings of the moment are always displaced, often painfully, into subsequent and ongoing refigurings. This is to be distinguished from mere repetition, an oscillation between mastery and slavery, activity and passivity, in that the passage of time makes simple repetition impossible—at least for the ideally imaginative mind, if not for Martha Ray as she is described to us. It is also quite different from the experience of the city, in that here the individual mind itself is at all time cooperative in administering such adjustments and corrections as occur. The forms which come into being are not prefigured by others, and are integrally educative rather than merely habit-forming.

This acceptance of antithesis helps to explain the presence of what is often felt to be a confusion in Wordsworth's epistemology. *The Prelude* presents a whole range of formulations of the mind-world relation, varying from active mind (and passive nature) to active nature (and passive mind), with consequent variations in the attribution of the 'real'. Thus the poet is unsure whether he has "transferr'd / His own enjoyments" to nature in a process of anthropomorphism, or whether he really has "convers'd / With things that really are" (II, 410 f.). At one moment his figured forms are the products of "deep analogies by thought supplied" (III, 122), at another they result from "Nature," which "Thrusts forth upon the senses" (XIII, 86) what is to be seen. At other times, correspondingly, some kind of mediation between these two positions is proposed. Outward form is "to the pleasure of the human mind / What passion makes it," but outward things have at the same time a "passion in themselves" which "intermingles" with man's activities (XII, 286–93). Thus there is produced

> A balance, an ennobling interchange
> Of action from within and from without,
> The excellence, pure spirit, and best power
> Both of the object seen, and eye that sees.
>
> (XII, 376–9)

These various positions, and the various permutations possible between them, would clearly make no sense as an attempt to propose a stable theoretical description of perception, one true for all places and at all times, and indeed for all people. All Romantic epistemology is basically synthetic, positing the cooperation of mind and world in the act of seeing and knowing; but it must be stressed that Wordsworth's version of the balance is actually an *interchange* through time, a process of which no one extrapolated moment or incident is properly representative. There is no privileged figuring of the real, which becomes an objective standard of normalcy; there is only a *series* of figurings, wherein a whole set of positions will be taken up from time to time, rising to vanish like clouds in the sky, and living on in the modified figures of the imaginative memory.

This formulation sheds new light on the problem . . . of how communication can take place, and consensus be established, in a world which may be composed of unstable personal configurations, companionable forms only of the isolated single mind and the projected receiver of its messages. We might infer from the Wordsworthian model, as I have described it, that if a series of positions are occupied at different times by the same mind, then all other minds (readers) might be expected to occupy similar positions at some time in the cycle of their experiences. Thus we might come to understand the transcendental structure of our minds as held in common with that of the poet, irrespective of the particular objects which we happen to relate to the particular dispositions of the mind within that structure. If we all go through the cycle of activity and passivity in our relations to the environment, then we hold that cycle in common even as no two people need be at the same point at the same time. We can thus contemplate the joys we cannot share, with something which may not improperly be called 'joy'. Further, as long as the process itself continues to occur, the particular deviations toward the extremes of mastery and slavery which it must include have no critical significance. They cannot solidify into a mystification of the 'real' as long as they are consistently dispersed by the figures which succeed them, and are never controlled by a single person or faction.

The above explanation, if it were applicable, would solve both the question of what different minds may hold in common (given that they cannot be assumed to 'see' the same 'objects'), and the ethical predicament of how we should respond to our world and to each other. What is fascinating about Wordsworth, however, is that at the same time as he affords us the materials to come up with explanatory models such as the above, he incorporates an insistence on the contextual considerations which must qualify or even spoil the prospect of such a model ever being adopted as practicable. He is in fact both prophetic and descriptive; he senses the urgent import of the ideally imaginative vision because he is so critically aware of what there is to threaten it, both in the world at large *and* in the aspiring individual mind, for they go together. The young man with his surplice performs the alienation whose effects he learns to deplore. A moral consensus is being sought in the mind of the sympathetic reader even as the very condition of that consensus is shown to be an empirical experience based in disturbance and disjunction. I think that there are two ways in which Wordsworth's discourse refuses its reader any position of acquiescent comfort. Firstly, there is the evidence that the insights of the poet as narrator will be felt to the full only by those sharers of a specific locale; a small community, a marginal economy, in a landscape sparse in its potential for being figured. Secondly, the whole model of adequation which the poet creates for himself out of the hard-won insights accompanying the experiences of consciousness, loss and transgression, is itself a figuring of the individual mind as it seeks to reflect on its own operation. This matters especially in Wordsworth since we are often shown that the dramatic speaker, the 'I', often functions by misapprehension and in solitude. There is thus no moment of perpetuated self-consciousness, no taking up of a position of authority, for the same reason that there is no 'spot' or fixed place which is not in fact defined in time. There is no perspective for commenting upon figures which is not itself a figure, and here we can suspect a source for the anxiety with which the Wordsworthian narrator sometimes turns to the brother poet, or to Dorothy. Kant had set himself a philosopher's task, and he had explained how experience is possible by reference to the tools the mind has to work with, the categories. The unspoken assumption behind this is that experience is *normal*. Wordsworth sets out from the other end, so to speak, and might have been happy to have been able to come to that conclusion. What troubles him is the suspicion that different minds are in fact operating with different tools, and tools either of their own mysterious making, or given them at second hand to be used at the service of their inventors. Wordsworth's urgent concern is certainly with the empirical. The sharing of the capacity to structure experience by space and time matters less to him than the use of that capacity in generous ways.

Apostrophe and Lyric Voice in *The Prelude*

Mary Jacobus

Looking back to the beginning of *The Prelude* [references are to the 1805 version], Book Seven starts by recalling the "dithyrambic fervour" with which it had opened. Named here as the "glad preamble," these introductory lines are recollected in terms at once of the natural Sublime and the Sublime of poetry itself:

> Five years are vanished since I first poured out . . .
> A glad preamble to this verse. I sang
> Aloud in dithyrambic fervour, deep
> But short-lived uproar, like a torrent sent
> Out of the bowels of a bursting cloud . . .
>
> (VII, 1–7)

Wordsworth's "torrent sent / Out of the bowels of a bursting cloud" is more than just a means of naturalizing the landscape of poetic inspiration; we recognize the source of a poetic Helicon. Geoffrey Hartman has suggested that *The Prelude* "can almost be said to begin with 'an Ode, in passion utter'd' " (V, 97). Though he does not enlarge on this connection between the "glad preamble" and the apocalyptic blast heard in the shell of Book Five, his allusion to the ode form is worth pursuing. The torrent of eloquence here has quite specific associations with the Sublime or Pindaric and (by popular misconception) "irregular" ode, certainly the highest form of lyric poetry for the eighteenth century, and the one in which the poet was

From *Lyric Poetry: Beyond New Criticism.* © 1985 by Cornell University Press.

also thought to speak most directly in his own voice. Translating Horace's praise of Pindar in one of his own *Pindarique Odes*, Cowley had written:

> *Pindars unnavigable Song*
> Like a swoln *Flood* from some steep *Mountain* pours along,
>   The *Ocean* meets with such a *Voice*
> From his enlarged *Mouth*, as drowns the *Oceans* noise.
>
> So *Pindar* does new *Words* and *Figures* roul
> Down his impetuous *Dithyrambic Tide*

As Cowley notes, the "*Dithyrambic Tide*" of Pindaric eloquence has its dangers, "for it is able to drown any *Head* that is not strong built and well *ballasted*." Wordsworth too may have glimpsed these dangers. Voice not only drowns the ocean's noise, but threatens to drown the reader too, and perhaps even the writer himself. Keeping one's head above water may even mean shutting one's ears. One might contrast also the torrent of words in the "glad preamble" with Wordsworth's invocation to the "steady cadence" of the River Derwent in Book One, which at once "composes" the infant's thoughts, and, in another sense, the entire poem. Did Wordsworth, perhaps, finding his own dithyrambic tide unnavigable, prefer to emphasize not the voice of the Sublime but the voice of Nature?

There are good reasons for this retreat from the Sublime. Cowley goes on to observe of Pindar's Dithyrambics that they were "*Hymns* made in honour of *Bacchus* . . . a bold, free, enthusiastical kind of Poetry, as of men inspired by *Bacchus*, that is, *Half-Drunk*." Remembering himself as a young poet in the throes of composition, Wordsworth speaks of hushing his voice and "composing" his gait so that passers-by wouldn't suppose him mad ("crazed in brain," IV, 116–20); "kindled with the stir, / The fermentation and the vernal heat / Of poesy" (IV, 93–95), he too is like one half-drunk. At Cambridge, youthful intoxication took the form of getting drunk in Milton's rooms. Apostrophe and libation blend in a heady brew: "O temperate bard!",

> I to thee
> Poured out libations, to thy memory drank
> Within my private thoughts, till my brain reeled,

Never so clouded by the fumes of wine
Before that hour, or since.
(III, 303–7)

Drinking to Milton's memory takes on an aspect at once sublime
and bacchic—inebriated with his poetry while disrespectful of Milton's own temperance. Milton himself comes to mind in this context
not only as the bard of temperance but as the poet most obsessed
with the terror of bacchic orgies, whose own apostrophe to Urania
at the start of Book Seven of *Paradise Lost*—clearly in Wordsworth's
mind as he wrote his opening to Book Seven of *The Prelude*—invokes
protection against just such a Comus-like crew of drunken revelers.

Wordsworth could praise Milton for "a voice whose sound was
like the sea" ("Milton," line 1)—a voice, presumably, in which all
others would be lost; but Milton's own anxiety was that his voice
would be drowned by savage clamor and the poet dismembered,
Orpheus-like, by hordes of Thracian women under the influence of
their bacchic cult. Wordsworth himself had translated this part of
the Orpheus and Eurydice story from Virgil's *Georgic* IV in 1788,
and it is hard to imagine that the legend can have been absent from
his mind either at the time of the original literary orgy in Milton's
rooms or later, when recollected in *The Prelude*. The figure used by
Cowley of the Pindaric Sublime ("it is able to drown any *Head* that
is not strong built and well *ballasted*") coincides with the traditional
figure of the poet's voice being drowned by barbarous dissonance,
and his severed head borne down the flood. Both appear to be articulations of the dread that poetic individuality might be lost—
whether by being subsumed into the Sublime or by being dispersed
into the meaningless multiplicity of "clamor." The orphic fantasy
might be said to involve for Wordsworth, as for Milton, the threat
that discomposing bacchic dithyrambs, or possession by the voices
of others, would lead to the poet's dismemberment.

One safeguard against such imaginary dismemberment is provided by the compensating fantasy of fully naturalized orphic song.
As Frances Ferguson aptly writes, the dying head gives nature a
speaking voice ("Ah! poor Eurydice, it feebly cried; / Eurydice, the
moaning banks replied"). For her, the echoic structure is that of
epitaph; but one might also see in it the Wordsworthian desire to
appropriate the speaking voice of Nature in an attempt to render his
own imperishable. Drowned neither by the voice of the Sublime—

Milton's voice—nor by the clamor of all the other voices by which the poet risks being possessed, the voice of Nature permits a loss of individuality which is at once safe and unifying. In Nature, the poet can take refuge against dismemberment.

If the poet's urgent need to constitute himself as a poet leads him to the dithyrambic fervor of the "glad preamble," self-preservation throws him back on naturalized song. On the one hand, the torrential or oceanic voices of past poets; on the other, the murmurings of the Derwent which assimilate the poet's voice to Nature and so preserve it. The ode-like, inspirational passion of the "glad preamble" ultimately "vex[es] its own creation" (I, 47), its redundant energy disrupting the flow of river and memory. By contrast, the fiction of a poetry that originates in Nature, like the voice of the Derwent, ensures continuity while providing a safely trans-subjective voice in which the poet's own can be merged. Wordsworth can claim not simply that Nature speaks through him, but that he speaks with Nature's own voice. The characteristic alternations in *The Prelude*—between the uproarious waterspout and the murmuring stream, inspiration and reflection, invocation and narrative—become a sign of this tension between poetic self-assertion and self-immersion. Wordsworth's final sleight of hand may well be that of divesting himself of the Sublime altogether while investing it in Nature instead. One might argue that his counterpart to Milton's cosmic flight derives from the self-immersing Bard of Gray's "Pindaric Ode," who "spoke, and headlong from the mountain's height / Deep in the roaring tide . . . plunged to endless night" ("The Bard," lines 143–44)—an ostensibly suicidal loss of individual identity which at once destroys the poet's voice and vests Nature with those qualities (Voice or voices) dangerous to its survival. As we see in Book Thirteen, this leaves the poet free to take refuge in pastoral, the address of one poet-shepherd to another. If the ode is the sublime and therefore dangerous form of the lyric, then apostrophe could be said to be the figure which most completely characterizes the sublimity of the ode. *The Prelude* begins apostrophically, but ends by addressing the living—Dorothy and Coleridge—in a way designed to assimilate the poet to a safer pastoral community. It is this formal progression that most clearly marks the concession made by a poet whose lyric voice survives finally at the price of renouncing the Sublime altogether. Paradoxically, only by making the torrential and uproarious voice

of inspiration that of Nature itself can Wordsworth sustain a voice
of his own.

II

> *Apostrophe!* we thus address
> More things than I should care to guess.
> Apostrophe! I did invoke
> Your figure even as I spoke.
> [John Hollander]

Apostrophe, as Jonathan Culler has observed, is an embarrass-
ment. Regularly ignored by writers on the ode, it might be seen "as
the figure of all that is most radical, embarrassing, pretentious, and
mystificatory in the lyric." Critics turn away from it as it turns away
from the discourse in which it is embedded; *apo-strophe*—literally, a
turning away, the abrupt transition which, as Cowley puts it in his
1656 Preface, takes the Pindaric ode out of "the common Roads, and
ordinary Tracks of *Poesie*. . . . The digressions are many, and sudden,
and sometimes long, according to the fashion of all *Lyriques*, and of
Pindar above all men living." Regarded as a digressive form, a sort
of interruption, excess, or redundance, apostrophe in *The Prelude*
becomes the signal instance of the rupture of the temporal scheme
of memory by the time of writing. Wordsworth's "two consciousnesses" (II, 32) can then be seen as a division, not simply between
me-now and me-then, but between discursive time and narrative
time—a radical discontinuity which ruptures the illusion of sequen-
tiality and insists, embarrassingly, on self-presence and voice; insists
too that invocation itself may be more important than what is invoked. "Apostrophe! I did invoke / Your figure even as I spoke"
is a joke that accurately mimes the bringing into being of the poet's
voice by way of what it addresses. If apostrophe's characteristic function is to invoke the Muse, it is also, ultimately, a form of self-
constituting self-address: "To my soul I say, 'I recognise thy glory' "
(VI, 531–32). The question of the poet's vocation, translated into
invocation, becomes the question of poetic voice. Like Imagination
in Book Six, voice halts the poet in his tracks, privileging self-address
over narrating the past. The opening apostrophe of the "glad preamble" may constitute Wordsworth as a poet but, in doing so, it loses
hold of his subject; there is always this incompatibility between the

lyric voice of *The Prelude* and its much-desired, "distracting" epic progress—an incompatibility which typically presents itself as a problem of redundance. Voice usurps on the ceaselessly-murmuring Derwent, making the poet himself the interpreter of his poem.

The "glad preamble" initiates not only *The Prelude*, but the problem of its composition. The erratic progress to which the opening lines of Book Seven allude (" 'twas not long / Ere the interrupted strain broke forth once more . . . then stopped for years," VII, 9–11) may be nothing other than the symptom of Wordsworth's anxiety about writing a long poem. Only in Book Twelve, looking back from a completed poem, can Wordsworth retrospectively see the image of a longed-for completeness in the stream that has been traced from darkness (XIII, 172–80). But perhaps the "glad preamble" should in the last resort be read, not simply as a dramatization of Wordsworth's anxiety about his poetic undertaking or as a record of the fluctuations of inspiration, but rather as a propitiatory gesture that frees the poet from the "burthen of [his] own unnatural self" and, in doing so, from the burdensome past of poetry. *The Prelude's* opening apostrophe to the breeze would then become an image of liberation which, though predicated on the novelty of self-presence to one "not used to make / A present joy the matter of [his] song" (I, 55–56), is directed ultimately at sloughing off his poetic precursors or consciousness of the past:

> O welcome messenger! O welcome friend!
> A captive greets thee, coming from a house
> Of bondage, from yon city's walls set free,
> A prison where he hath been long immured.
> Now I am free, enfranchised and at large,
> May fix my habitation where I will. . . .
>   I breathe again—
> Trances of thought and mountings of the mind
> Come fast upon me. It is shaken off,
> As by a miraculous gift 'tis shaken off,
> That burthen of my own unnatural self
>   (I, 5–10, 19–23)

The poet's breathing and the breeze are at once the breath of pure unconstructed sound ('O' or voice) and a prison-break, an escape from the confines of memory and self-consciousness. In the same way, apostrophe itself breaks off from the demands of narrative as a moment of lyric redundance or inspired escape. The "vital breeze" becomes "A tempest, a redundant energy, / Vexing its own creation" (I, 46–47), just as in the opening lines of Book Seven the grove "tossing its dark boughs in sun and wind— / Spreads through me a commotion like its own" (VII, 51–52). This tempest or commotion is not exactly a "corresponding mild creative breeze" (I, 43); it is more a vexation or a kind of uneasiness. The effect is that of voice itself, perceived as an interruption of the past from the present.

Wordsworth comments of the "glad preamble," "My own voice cheared me, and, far more, the mind's / Internal echo of the imperfect sound" (I, 64–65). The appeal to voice might usually be thought of as having the function of making the self whole. Whereas writing disperses, voice unifies, providing the illusion of a single origin and temporal unity (no "two consciousnesses" here). Yet in this instance, Wordsworth writes of the doubling effect whereby the sound of his own voice has an internal echo, and one which, unlike echo as usually figured, perfects rather than incompletely repeats "the imperfect sound"; it is voice here that functions like echo, since speech is imagined as secondary in its attempt to represent the silence of self-present meaning in consciousness. At this point it seems worth digressing to consider some of the more problematic aspects of the Romantic conception of voice. A small book by Francis Berry, *Poetry and the Physical Voice* (1962), brings to light the hidden implications of Wordsworth's position. Like Wordsworth, Berry appears to insist on the primacy of voice over writing (seeing the letter simply as a representation of sound), and his book laments the debasing of language as a mere means of communication, or "instrument." Yet this distinction between language as instrument and the poetic use of language as "agent" proves oddly difficult to sustain.

As Wordsworth had been, Berry too is anxious to restore to poetic voice the musicality which he believes once to have been synonymous with poetry itself. But even Wordsworth no longer insists on "feigning that [his] works were composed to the music of the harp or lyre," happily substituting "nothing more than an animated or impassioned recitation." Berry's terms—pitch, duration, volume, timbre, and so on—emphasize the sound of vocal "music" to a degree never risked by Wordsworth himself. In doing so, however, they uncover the underlying myth of voice of which Wordsworth's is a less extreme version; that is, the myth of the "inner ear" (not a kind of memory but a kind of hearing) which leads us to suppose, according to Berry, that though "modern poets compose silently . . . in composing they record what they are inwardly experiencing as vocal sound, usually their own voices however idealized. . . . we could say they record the double experiences of hearing *and* saying"; this is what Wordsworth had called "the mind's internal echo of the imperfect sound," likewise surrendering to an auditory myth of self-presence. But there follows for Berry an altogether less composing notion, that of the poet as "a person obsessed, scored and spoored by vocal linguistic sound"; "or, put another way, he is *possessed* by vocal sound as a man was said to be possessed by devils." What it amounts to is that voice, instead of bringing reassurance ("my own voice cheared me") by guaranteeing the existence of a unified consciousness, can equally take on the demonic aspect of possession. Whose are the voices the poet hears? Not necessarily his own, after all.

In the light of such demonic vocalism, Berry's notion of individuated voice breaks down. His insistence that the attentive ("listening") reader can recover or reconstruct the unique and authentic voices of, say, Tennyson, Milton, or—presumably—Wordsworth on the evidence of "the printed signs on the page" is revealed as a fiction. Calling the self into being through apostrophe becomes rather a matter of calling another into being; perhaps an "authorial" voice, but equally, the variety of haunting, threatening, nightmarish, or apocalyptic voices heard throughout *The Prelude* in "the voice / Of mountain echoes" (I, 389–90), or in "Black drizzling drags that spake . . . As if a voice were in them" (VI, 563–4), or the "voice that cried / To the whole city, 'Sleep no more!' " (X, 76–77), or in a shell that broadcasts "voices more than all the winds"—the voice of "a god, yea many gods" (V, 107–8). The voice is always a doubling of self, and more often a multiplication or alienation. Berry's view of poetic language as agent, then, turns out to be characterized not by the individuality of the writer but by something closer to the supernatural—the gift of tongues or hearing voices ("he is *possessed* by vocal sound"). Conceived as a man more vocal than other men, the poet becomes an echo-chamber for all those voices heard while boat-stealing, descending the Vale of Gondo, unable to sleep in Paris after the September Massacres, or in the Arab Dream. They speak through him, so that far from attesting to unity of origin or a stable identity, voice comes to imply all the destabilizing multiplicity of plural (or ancestral) voices—much as the composing "voice" of the

Derwent can become the discomposing voice of inspired poetry, "the voice / Which roars along the bed of Jewish song," or the Miltonic "trumpet-tones of harmony that shake / Our shores in England" (V, 203–4, 206–7). Given these transformations, Wordsworth's quest turns out not to be for an individual voice so much as for a transcendental one.

The apostrophic moments in Book One of *The Prelude* are, typically, callings into being of supernatural powers:

> Wisdom and spirit of the universe,
> Thou soul that art the eternity of thought,
> That giv'st to forms and images a breath
> And everlasting motion . . .
>
> (I, 427–31)

> Ye presences of Nature, in the sky
> Or on the earth, ye visions of the hills
> And souls of lonely places . . .
>
> (I, 490–92)

Wordsworth's invocations to the Muse summon up spirits, presences, souls—the supernatural machinery of an unexorcized Nature, arising in the same breath as winds, hills, solitude. If Shelley demands of the wind, "Be thou me, impetuous one!" Wordsworth could be said to ask of Nature to give his voice whatever haunts and denatures landscape; whatever puts the individual origin of voice most in question. The Eolian fantasy so beloved of Romantic poets, after all, is nothing more or less than the wish for the trans-subjective instrumentality which Berry would repress if he could, but fails ultimately to exorcize. Wordsworth's apostrophes to breezes, brooks, and groves, in which he wishes for himself "a music and a voice harmonious as your own" (XI, 20–21), are the equivalent of asking to be played on too. The distinction which Wordsworth himself would have endorsed, between language as instrument (or, as he calls it himself, "counter-spirit") and language as agent, falls away to leave only breezes or breathings through the poet, "obedient as a lute / That waits upon the touches of the wind" (III, 137–8). Subsumed into transcendental Nature, the poet's voice becomes orphic rather than bacchic, banishing rough music with the myth of natural harmony. Nature steps in to de-demonize voice, turning possession into Eolianism and sanctifying vocalism as "Eolian visitations" (I, 104).

Instead of the voice of the poet, we have the voice of poetry—that is, Nature. In order to achieve this status for his poetry, Wordsworth has to eschew the very fiction of individual voice which is central to Romantic conceptions of the poet. The transcendental defends against possession, but it also takes away the poet's most distinctive and sought-after personal property, the voice that differentiates him from his predecessors, and from Milton in particular. That, perhaps, may be the trade-off—since not to be either Milton or unlike Milton is in effect to lose the Miltonic voice as well as one's own in the impersonally oceanic voice of Nature, thereby drowning the potentially ventriloquizing voices of the past in "A waterspout from heaven" (VII, 9).

III

What is involved for Wordsworth in sound itself? And what is the relation of voice to writing? The aftermath of the "glad preamble" turns out to be largely one of discouragement: "the harp / Was soon defrauded" (I, 104–5) and the hope of fixing "in a visible home... those phantoms of conceit, / That had been floating loose about so long" (I, 129–31) was not to be fulfilled. The disembodied "phantoms of conceit" remain unrepresented, perhaps unrepresentable. A fragment from the *Peter Bell* MS, possibly an early attempt at an introduction to the two-part *Prelude*, had explored the problem of representation in terms directly relevant to the random vocalizings of the "glad preamble":

> nor had my voice
> Been silent—oftentimes had I burst forth
> In verse which with a strong and random light
> Touching an object in its prominent parts
> Created a memorial which to me
> Was all sufficient, and, to my own mind
> Recalling the whole picture, seemed to speak
> An universal language. Scattering thus
> In passion many a desultory sound,
> I deemed that I had adequately cloathed
> Meanings at which I hardly hinted, thoughts
> And forms of which I scarcely had produced
> A monument and arbitrary sign.

Bursting forth in verse becomes the equivalent of a private mnemonic; "to my *own* mind / Recalling the whole picture," the voice only "*seemed* to speak / An universal language." Writing to Godwin in 1800, Coleridge had asked, "Is *thinking* impossible without arbitrary signs? &—how far is the word 'arbitrary' a misnomer?" If Coleridge seems to want to destroy "the old antithesis of *Words & Things*, elevating . . . words into Things, & living Things too," Wordsworth seems to be suggesting that at best poetry can produce "A monument and arbitrary sign" for thought; and at worst, make only desultory sounds. This is the Eolian fantasy demystified, and along with it there collapses the entire Romantic fallacy of spontaneous lyric utterance, whether heard or overheard. In another fragment, Wordsworth alludes to "slow creation" imparting "to speach / Outline and substance." This sounds like fixing phantoms of conceit in a visible home, or writing poetry. It is as if representation only begins at the point where Eolianism—the fiction of unmediated expression—is eschewed; or perhaps, Wordsworth seems to imply, thinking can begin only where the monuments and arbitrary signs of language take over from sound (pure voice or breath) and speech (pure presence). In any event, it is clear that writing, the permanent record of thought, involves both the muting of voice—a kind of deafness—and the death of presence.

No wonder, then, that Eolianism pervades *The Prelude*; it is Wordsworth's defense against that inability to hear oneself think (or speak) involved in writing itself. Going back to the opening of Book Seven, we find Wordsworth experiencing "Something that fits me for the poet's task" in the infectious "commotion" of his favorite grove, "Now tossing its dark boughs in sun and wind" (VII, 50–53). Presumably both grove and poet make a composing noise much like the one that is wasted on the deaf Dalesman, though not on his peaceful grave, memorialized in Wordsworth's final "Essay on Epitaphs":

> And yon tall pine-tree, whose composing sound
> Was wasted on the good Man's living ear,
> Hath now its own peculiar sanctity;
> And at the touch of every wandering breeze
> Murmurs not idly o'er his peaceful grave.

The Dalesman's epitaph is "A monument and arbitrary sign" masquerading as the sound of murmuring trees, alias the composing sound of the poet's own voice. Why does the pine-tree murmur "not idly"? Is it because the entire epitaph, though ostensibly commemorating a man for whom the mountain vale was soundless and the storm-tossed landscape "silent as a picture"—for whom all voices save those of books were unheard—actually celebrates the poet's own aural imagination as a means of denying the soundlessness of writing? The poet himself, Wordsworth implies, is not only murmurous but has inward ears that can hear; this is what makes him a poet. Imagined sound becomes a way to repress or deny writing and undo death. If a monument marks the site of a grave, voice—"breathings for incommunicable powers" (III, 188)—gives evidence of a poet's enduring life. For the poet, Wordsworth argues covertly, there can be no such thing as silence, but only, as in the Dalesman's epitaph, "audible seclusions." The soundless world of the Dalesman's solitude and death is one that speaks to him. So much so that in *The Prelude* a moment of visionary seeing is as likely as not to be one of hearing, an attempt to communicate "what e'er there is of power in sound / To breathe an elevated mood":

> I would stand
> Beneath some rock, listening to sounds that are
> The ghostly language of the ancient earth,
> Or make their dim abode in distant winds.
> Thence did I drink the visionary power.
>
> (II, 326–30)

Visionary power—"by form / Or image unprofaned"—is a heightened sense of hearing which makes language into something ghostly, nonreferential, ancient, and without origin, like the homeless voice of waters in the Snowdon episode. Along with Francis Berry, Wordsworth wants to believe that the poet hears voices as well as speaking with tongues; but what he most desires to hear are the unheard sighings or breathings that writing ("arbitrary signs") must repress. This is the other side of babble, or Babel, the nonlinguistic murmur of a composing voice that may be the poet's as he saunters "like a river murmuring" (IV, 110) or, equally, invoked as that of the Derwent ("O, Derwent, murmuring stream," V, 509), but is above all that of a unified poetic presence that has no need of discourse.

Wordsworth's definitive statement of the ear's power occurs in his "musical" ode, "On the Power of sound" (1828). As the preposterous "argument" puts it, "The Ear [is] addressed, as occupied by a spiritual functionary, in communion with sounds, individual, or combined in studied harmony." The ode is all apostrophe, all voice, all ear:

> a Spirit aërial
> Informs the cell of Hearing, dark and blind;
> Intricate labyrinth, more dread for thought
> To enter than oracular cave
>
> (lines 3–6)

The ear becomes the prime organ of vision, making audible "Ye Voices, and ye shadows / And Images of voice" (lines 33–34). The poem's function is both to invoke Spirit (ear) and Muse (voice); or "the mind's / Internal echo of the imperfect sound." As John Hollander's account of the poem has shown, the ear is a place of echo and reverberation, sounding and re-sounding, a cave, a "strict passage," a maze, a temple, a vault, a hollow place where music is made as well as heard. Like the shell, whether a poeticism for the lute or the Romanticized seashell, it is both sounded on and sounds, combining the orphic properties of a stringed instrument and the dionysian properties of a wind instrument. In effect, it is nothing less than the ear of God. Wordsworth's originary myth of voice ("A Voice to Light gave Being," line 209) is also an apocalyptic one: "A Voice shall . . . sweep away life's visionary stir" (lines 211–2). Compare the dual functions of music and harmony in *The Prelude*, one to build up, the other to destroy; though "The mind of man is framed even like the breath / And harmony of music" (lines 351–2), the shell's "loud prophetic blast of harmony" (V, 96) in the Arab dream announces the end of the world, and the sublime of Revolutionary terror is accompanied by "Wild blasts of music" (X, 419). Music can both frame and unframe, compose and discompose. Wordsworth's unstated argument in "On the Power of Sound" is to reconcile this dual aspect of harmony, claiming that even after earth is dust and the heavens dissolved, "her stay / Is in the WORD, that shall not pass away" (lines 223–4). His ode is the optimistic, orthodox Christian sequel to the Arab dream, revised not to foretell "Destruction to the children of the earth" (V, 98) but rather to prophesy salvation of and through the Word. As the type of the divine fiat, poetry itself is guaranteed survival—the consolatory message unavailable to the Arab or the dreamer in Book Five of *The Prelude*—by means of its transformation into the transcendental, imperishable

"WORD." Poetic utterance now promises "to finish doubt and dim foreseeing" (line 211), dependent no longer on "books" (the materiality of stone or shell), but on the special harmony of Christian assurance or faith in life—and therefore faith in hearing—beyond death. This is a word that can continue to hear itself and be heard even after the apocalypse.

The guaranteeing of poetry as "WORD" (voice transcendentalized as Logos) in "On the Power of Sound" reveals one function of sound, and particularly of voice, in *The Prelude* itself. What the deaf Dalesman can "hear" are the immortal voices of the poets, secured against "imperfection and decay":

> Song of the muses, sage historic tale
> Science severe, or word of holy writ
> Announcing immortality and joy
> To the assembled spirits of the just,
> From imperfection and decay secure.
> [*Excursion*, VII, 450–4]

After the death of the poet, there still remains immortal verse. In lines like these, Wordsworth uses silent reading to free poetry from the monumentality and arbitrary signs of death. Disembodied sound— "The ghostly language of the ancient earth"—comes to be the archetype of poetry. In this light, the "glad preamble" might be seen not only as a means of calling both poet and voice into being, but also as a way to fantasize their transcendence of material representation. In *The Prelude* Wordsworth had hoped vainly "that with a frame of outward life" he might "fix in a visible home . . . those phantoms of conceit / That had been floating loose about so long" (I, 128–31). How are we to read this self-proclaimed failure to fix the insubstantial (and hence imperishable) "phantoms of conceit"? The longing "To brace myself to some determined aim" (I, 124) is synonymous in *The Prelude* with the epic enterprise itself, yet the poem finally evades even this enterprise by substituting the "WORD"—lasting, but inaudible except to the mind—for an epic theme. It is left celebrating the spirit or "voice" of poetry instead of the form. Like the cuckoo, "No bird, but an invisible thing, / A voice, a mystery" ("To the cuckoo," lines 15–16), poet as well as poem becomes unavailable, "dispossesse[d] . . . almost of a corporeal existence." An extended personal lyric, *The Prelude* is redeemed from time and death by the unheard voice of the poet, or, as Wordsworth calls it, the Imagination, its declared subject. The entire poem becomes an apostrophe or "prelude" designed to constitute the poet and to permit Wordsworth himself to join the ranks of Homer, the great thunderer, and the Bible, Milton, and even the ballad, as Voice rather than voice, Poetry rather than individual poet; that is, the Voice of Poetry which re-sounds not only in the ears of the living but in the ears of the deaf.

Chronology

1770   Born April 7 at Cockermouth in Cumberland.
1778   Death of mother, Ann Wordsworth.
1779   Enters school near Esthwaite Lake in the Lake Country.
1783   Death of father, John Wordsworth.
1787–91 Attends St. John's College, Cambridge University.
1790   Walking tour of France, Germany, and Switzerland.
1791   Walking tour of North Wales, where he ascends Mount Snowdon.
1791–92 Residence in France, where he associates with moderate faction of the Revolution. Love affair with Annette Vallon. Birth of their daughter, Anne-Caroline.
1793   Publication of *An Evening Walk* and *Descriptive Sketches*.
1795   Death of college friend, Raisley Calvert, whose legacy enables Wordsworth to devote himself to his poetry.
1795–98 Settles with his sister Dorothy first at Racedown, and then at Alfoxden. In 1797–98, he is constantly in the company of Samuel Taylor Coleridge.
1798   In September, *Lyrical Ballads* is published, with Coleridge.
1798–99 Winters with Dorothy at Goslar in Germany.
1799   Moves with Dorothy to Dove Cottage, Grasmere, where he writes *The Prelude* in its first version, in two parts.
1800   Second edition of *Lyrical Ballads*, with "Preface" added.
1802   Marries Mary Hutchinson.
1805   Death of his brother, John Wordsworth, who goes down with his ship in February. *The Prelude*, in thirteen books, is finished, but the poet chooses not to publish it.
1807   Publishes *Poems in Two Volumes*.
1810–12 Rift with Coleridge; subsequent friendship is never the same.

1813–42   Becomes government tax collector for Westmoreland. Lives at Rydal Mount, near Ambleside.

1814   Publishes *The Excursion.*

1835   Dorothy's madness begins.

1843   Becomes Poet Laureate.

1850   Dies April 23 at Rydal Mount. *The Prelude*, in fourteen books, is published posthumously.

Contributors

HAROLD BLOOM, Sterling Professor of the Humanities at Yale University, is the author of *The Anxiety of Influence*, *Poetry and Repression*, and many other volumes of literary criticism. His forthcoming study, *Freud: Transference and Authority*, attempts a full-scale reading of all of Freud's major writings. A MacArthur Prize Fellow, he is general editor of five series of literary criticism published by Chelsea House.

WILLIAM EMPSON was Professor of English at the University of Sheffield. His celebrated criticism includes *Seven Types of Ambiguity*, *Some Versions of Pastoral*, *The Structure of Complex Words*, and *Milton's God*. His work also includes several volumes of verse.

DONALD DAVIE, a poet and scholar, is Professor of English at Stanford University. He is the author of *Articulate Energy: An Inquiry into the Syntax of English Poetry* and *Purity of Diction in English Verse* as well as many books of poetry.

GEOFFREY HARTMAN, Karl Young Professor of English and Comparative Literature at Yale, is the author of *The Unmediated Vision* and *Wordsworth's Poetry*. In addition to his work on Wordsworth, his books include *Beyond Formalism* and *Saving the Text*.

HERBERT LINDENBERGER is Professor of Humanities at Stanford University and the author of *On Wordsworth's* Prelude.

M. H. ABRAMS, the most distinguished living scholar of Romanticism, is Class of 1916 Professor of English at Cornell University. His masterwork is *The Mirror and the Lamp*, the definitive study of Romantic critical theory, which ought to be read in conjunction with his other major books, *Natural Supernaturalism* and *The Correspondent Breeze*.

RICHARD J. ONORATO is Associate Professor of English at Brandeis University and the author of *The Character of the Poet: Wordsworth in* The Prelude.

ROBERT YOUNG is an editor of *The Oxford Literary Review* and is Lecturer in English at the University of Southampton.

DAVID E. SIMPSON is a Fellow of King's College, Cambridge, and the author of *Irony and Authority in Romantic Poetry* and *Wordsworth and the Figurings of the Real*.

MARY JACOBUS is Professor of English at Cornell University and the author of *Tradition and Experiment in Wordsworth's Lyrical Ballads*. Her work also includes essays on Romantic prose and feminist literary criticism.

Bibliography

Abrams, M. H., ed. *Wordsworth: A Collection of Critical Essays*. Englewood Cliffs, N. J.: Prentice-Hall, 1972.

Abrams, M. H., Stephen Gill, and Jonathan Wordsworth, eds. *The Prelude 1799, 1805, 1850*. New York: W. W. Norton & Co., 1979.

Arac, Jonathan. "Bounding Lines: *The Prelude* and Critical Revision." *Boundary 2* 7, no. 3 (1979): 31–48.

Averill, James H. *Wordsworth and the Poetry of Human Suffering*. Ithaca: Cornell University Press, 1980.

Baker, Jeffrey. *Time and Mind in Wordsworth's Poetry*. Detroit, Mich.: Wayne State University Press, 1980

Beer, John Bernard. *Wordsworth and the Human Heart*. New York: Columbia University Press, 1978.

Bialostosky, Don H. *Making Tales: The Poetics of Wordsworth's Narrative Experiments*. Chicago: The University of Chicago Press, 1984.

Byatt, Antonia Susan. *Wordsworth and Coleridge in Their Time*. London: Nelson, 1970.

Chandler, James K. *Wordsworth's Second Nature: A Study of the Poetry and Politics*. Chicago: The University of Chicago Press, 1984.

Davies, Hunter. *William Wordsworth: A Biography*. London: Weidenfield & Nicolson, 1980.

Devlin, David Douglas. *Wordsworth and the Poetry of Epitaphs*. London: Macmillan & Co., 1980.

———. *Wordsworth and the Art of Prose*. London: Macmillan & Co., 1983.

Ellis, David. *Wordsworth, Freud, and the Spots of Time*. Cambridge: Cambridge University Press, 1985.

Ferguson, Frances. *Wordsworth: Language as Counter-Spirit*. New Haven: Yale University Press, 1977.

Ferry, David. *The Limits of Mortality: An Essay on Wordsworth's Major Poems*. Middletown, Conn.: Wesleyan University Press, 1959.

Gerard, Albert S. *English Romantic Poetry: Ethos, Structure, and Symbol in Coleridge, Wordsworth, Shelley, and Keats*. Berkeley and Los Angeles: University of California Press, 1968.

Gill, Stephen, ed. *William Wordsworth*. New York: Oxford University Press, 1984.

Gravil, Richard. "Wordsworth's Ontology of Love in *The Prelude*." *The Critical Quarterly* 16 (1974): 231–49.

Grob, Alan. *The Philosophic Mind: A Study of Wordsworth's Poetry and Thought 1797–1805*. Columbus: Ohio University Press, 1973.

Halliday, F. E. *Wordsworth and His World*. London: Thames & Hudson, 1970.

Hartman, Geoffrey. *Wordsworth's Poetry*. New Haven: Yale University Press, 1971.

———, ed. *New Perspectives on Coleridge and Wordsworth*. New York: Columbia University Press, 1972.

Haven, Raymond Dexter. *The Mind of a Poet*. Baltimore: The Johns Hopkins University Press, 1941.

Hayden, John O., ed. *The Poems of William Wordsworth*. New Haven: Yale University Press, 1981.

Heath, William. *Wordsworth and Coleridge: A Study of Their Literary Relations in 1801–1802*. New York: Oxford University Press, 1970.

Heffernan, James A. W. *William Wordsworth's Theory of Poetry: The Transforming Imagination*. Ithaca: Cornell University Press, 1969.

Hodgson, John A. *Wordsworth's Philosophical Poetry, 1797–1814*. Lincoln: University of Nebraska Press, 1980.

Jackson, Wallace. *The Probable and the Marvelous: Blake, Wordsworth, and the Eighteenth-Century Critical Tradition*. Athens: University of Georgia Press, 1978.

Jacobus, Mary. "Wordsworth and the Language of the Dream." *ELH* 46 (1979): 541–644.

Johnson, Lee M. *Wordsworth's Metaphysical Verse: Geometry, Nature, and Form*. Toronto: University of Toronto Press, 1982.

Johnston, Kenneth R. *Wordsworth and The Recluse*. New Haven: Yale University Press, 1984.

Jones, Henry John Franklin. *The Egotistical Sublime: A History of Wordsworth's Imagination*. London: Chatto & Windus, 1954.

King, Alexander. *Wordsworth and the Artist's Vision*. London: Athlone Press, 1966.

Lindenberger, Herbert. *On Wordsworth's* Prelude. Princeton: Princeton University Press, 1963.

Liu, Alan. " 'Shapeless Eagerness': The Genre of Revolution in Books 9–10 of *The Prelude.*" *Modern Language Quarterly* 43 (1982): 3–28.

McConnel, Frank D. *The Confessional Imagination: A Reading of Wordsworth's* Prelude. Baltimore: The Johns Hopkins University Press, 1974.

McFarland, Thomas. *Romanticism and the Forms of Ruin: Wordsworth, Coleridge, and the Modalities of Fragmentation*. Princeton: Princeton University Press, 1981.

Onorato, Richard J. *The Character of the Poet: Wordsworth in* The Prelude. Princeton: Princeton University Press, 1971.

Parrish, Stephen Maxfield, ed. *The Prelude, 1798–1799*. Ithaca: Cornell University Press, 1977.

Perkins, David. *The Quest for Permanence: The Symbolism of Wordsworth, Shelley, and Keats*. Cambridge: Harvard University Press, 1959.

―――. *Wordsworth and the Poetry of Sincerity*. Cambridge, Mass.: Belknap Press, 1964.

Peterfreund, Stuart. "*The Prelude*: Wordsworth's Metamorphic Epic." *Genre* 14 (1981): 441–72.

Pirie, David. *William Wordsworth: The Poetry of Grandeur and of Tenderness*. London: Methuen, 1982.

Reed, Mark L. *Wordsworth: The Chronology of the Middle Years, 1800–1815*. Cambridge: Harvard University Press, 1975.

Regueiro, Helen. *The Limits of Imagination: Wordsworth, Yeats, and Stevens*. Ithaca: Cornell University Press, 1976.

Rehder, Robert. *Wordsworth and the Beginnings of Modern Poetry*. Totowa, N. J.: Barnes & Noble, 1981.

Ricks, Christopher. "Wordsworth: 'A Pure Organic Pleasure from the Lines.' " In *The Force of Poetry*. Oxford: Clarendon Press, 1984.

Sheats, Paul D., ed. *The Poetical Works of Wordsworth*. Boston: Houghton Mifflin Co., 1982.

Sherry, Charles. *Wordsworth's Poetry of the Imagination*. Oxford: Clarendon Press, 1980.

Simpson, David E. *Wordsworth and the Figurings of the Real*. London: Macmillan & Co., 1982.

Spivak, Gayarti Chakravorty. "Sex and History in *The Prelude* (1805): Books Nine to Thirteen." *Texas Studies in Language and Literature* 23 (1981): 324–60.

Vogler, Thomas A. *Preludes to Vision: The Epic Venture in Blake, Wordsworth, Keats, and Hart Crane*. Berkeley and Los Angeles: University of California Press, 1971.

Watson, J. R. *Wordsworth's Vital Soul: The Sacred and the Profane in Wordsworth's Poetry*. London: Macmillan & Co., 1982.

Wesling, Donald. *Wordsworth and the Adequacy of Landscape*. London: Routledge & Kegan Paul, 1970.

Acknowledgments

"Introduction" (originally entitled "William Wordsworth: *The Prelude*") by Harold Bloom from *The Visionary Company* by Harold Bloom, © 1961 by Harold Bloom. Reprinted by permission.

"Sense in *The Prelude*" by William Empson from *The Structure of Complex Words* by William Empson, © 1951, 1952, 1977 by William Empson. Reprinted by permission of Chatto & Windus, Ltd. and Harvard University Press.

"Syntax in the Blank Verse of Wordsworth's *Prelude*" by Donald Davie from *Articulate Energy: An Inquiry into the Syntax of English Poetry* by Donald Davie, © 1955 by Donald Davie. Reprinted by permission of Routledge & Kegan Paul PLC.

"The Romance of Nature and the Negative Way" by Geoffrey Hartman from *The Unmediated Vision* by Geoffrey Hartman, © 1954 by Yale University and © 1982 by Geoffrey Hartman, and from *Wordsworth's Poetry 1787–1814* by Geoffrey Hartman, © 1964 by Yale University. Reprinted by permission of Yale University Press.

"The Structural Unit: 'Spots of Time' " by Herbert Lindenberger from *On Wordsworth's* Prelude by Herbert Lindenberger, © 1963 by Princeton University Press. Reprinted by permission of the publisher.

"Wordsworth's Long Journey Home" (originally entitled "The Idea of *The Prelude*" and "William Wordsworth: The Long Journey Home") by M. H. Abrams from *Natural Supernaturalism* by M. H. Abrams, © 1971 by W. W. Norton & Company, Inc. Reprinted by permission of W. W. Norton & Company, Inc.

"The Fiction of the Self" by Richard J. Onorato from *The Character of the Poet: Wordsworth in* The Prelude by Richard J. Onorato, © 1971 by Princeton University Press. Reprinted by permission of the publisher.

"The Eye and Progress of His Song: A Lacanian Reading of *The Prelude*" by Robert Young from *The Oxford Literary Review* 3, no. 3 (Spring 1979), © 1979 by *The Oxford Literary Review*. Reprinted by permission.

"The Spots of Time: Spaces for Refiguring" by David E. Simpson from *Wordsworth and the Figurings of the Real* by David E. Simpson, © 1982 by David E. Simpson. Reprinted by permission of Macmillan Publishers Ltd. and Humanities Press, Inc.

"Apostrophe and Lyric Voice in *The Prelude*" by Mary Jacobus from *Lyric Poetry: Beyond New Criticism*, edited by Chaviva Hosek and Patricia Parker, © 1985 by Cornell University Press. Reprinted by permission of Cornell University Press.

Index